COSPLAY

MARTIN PETERSEN

COSPLAY

Volume one

East Asian popular culture in a transnational perspective

A National Museum of Denmark Collection

University Press of Southern Denmark 2022

University of Southern Denmark Studies in History and Social Sciences Vol. 629
Layout and cover: Dorthe Møller, Unisats
Cover: Kami Renee. *High school of the Dead*. Photo: Julie Rønberg
Printed by Narayana Press

ISBN 978-87-408-3394-2

Cosplay is published with support from
Farumgaard-Fonden
Kulturministeriets Forskningspulje
National Museum of Denmark
Toyota-Fonden

University Press of Southern Denmark
55 Campusvej
DK-5230 Odense M
www.universitypress.dk

Distribution in the United States and Canada:
Independent Publishers Group
814 Franklin Street
Chicago, Il 60610
USA
www.ipgbook.com

Distribution in the United Kingdom:
Gazelle
White Cross Mills
Hightown
Lancaster
LA1 4 XS
U.K.
www.gazellebookservices.co.uk

Contents

Part Two:
Fan Productivity and Trans-Asian Media Referencing Among Danish Cosplayers 57

Part Three:
Interviews 101

Part Four:
Fan Productions 121

Conclusion 147

List of Illustrations 149

Introduction

Ending scenes. Beginnings: An ethnographic sketch

September, 2014. Marie has just re-watched her DVD with Hayao Miyazaki's *Howl's Moving Castle* (2004) made by Studio Ghibli. The anime (animated movie) left her emotional and on the verge of tears. It is a story about the young woman Sophie who is bewitched and transformed into an old woman. She encounters the wizard Howl. He is trying to intervene in the war between the kingdom Sophie comes from and the neighbouring kingdom. Sophie, Howl and their friends manage to bring an end to the war, and at the end of the story, Sophie and Howl travel in the air in a flying castle. Marie wants to make the costume worn by Sophie in this closing scene.

This starts an intense research of web sites for inspiration to style, design and fabrics. Marie reads interviews with the artist who designed the costumes for *Howl's Moving Castle*. She then turns to books on Victorian dressmaking. She is aiming for a style and look that will convey the atmosphere of airiness which she felt was so strongly present in the ending scene. All along, she is developing the ideas together with a friend, Himo. Himo makes the costume and character of Howl, the male protagonist in the closing scene.

The two friends go on a photo shoot with a photographer in a public park nearby the convention Dokumi in Düsseldorf, Germany. Here, they test out various locations and perspectives to create a photo, which recreates moments from the closing scene in an interpretation that brings out the airiness Marie experienced and felt when watching the anime.

This story sketches Marie's activities as a cosplayer and how she cosplayed Sophie in the closing scene from *Howl's Moving Castle*.

Apart from the Studio Ghibli anime, which is widely recognized by a Danish audience,[1] Marie is an avid consumer of Japanese manga (comics) and anime unfamiliar to the mainstream Danish consumer. This interest in media products from Japanese creative industries also spurs her on to read, watch and follow fan works and productions made globally, whether these are in the form of fan fiction, fan art or cosplay photography. From these interests she also moved into Korean popular culture and its fandoms – but that is another story. Like Marie and Himo's *Howl's Moving Castle* cosplay photo shoot, these creative fan products in various ways engage story worlds, characters and design from Japanese popular culture, not least manga, anime and video games.

The above is a portrait of a young, Danish female fan of Japanese anime, manga and other popular culture products from and related to Japan and how this interest is productive in bringing forth emotions, reflections and creative expressions. The portrait is based on a series of conversations and e-mail correspondence with Marie in 2014-2015. The portrait should not be seen as representative of cosplay, of Danish cosplay, of Danish cosplay in the mid-2010s or even of Marie's engagement with Japanese popular culture. Rather, it is but one story about how Marie was moved by an anime to make a cosplay – with all that 'the making of a cosplay' entails of dress making and collaboration with friends, pursuit of secondary references and spending an afternoon in front of a camera. In my conversations, interviews and observations on cosplay, this fan engagement was one common feature. In this sense, then, the story of Marie and Sophie speaks of Danish intimacies with Japanese popular culture – and how these intimacies turn into productivity.

1 The animation was screened in Danish movie theatres and widely distributed in stores and shops with DVDs.

At its core, this book attempts to arrive at an understanding of and give a presentation of the intimacy as it is experienced and lived out by Marie and her contemporaries; fellow cosplayers and fans of manga, anime, video games and the range of fan-based media, formats and genres that these are intimately intertwined with. The book is based on field-study mainly conducted in 2013-15 and qualitative interviews with a main focus on one male and four female Danish fans of Japanese popular culture who are all in their early 20s. A key part of this fieldwork research was an ongoing collaboration with especially three of these Danish informants in the making of the National Museum of Denmark permanent exhibition *Cosplayer! Manga Youth* (2015), for which I conceptualized the idea and was the curator. The exhibition also featured three Japanese cosplayers. I have to a great extent included the perspective of these Japanese informants throughout this volume. This is done to provide a comparative perspective and as way to contextualize Danish cosplay in the mid-2010s.

Contents

The present volume attempts to capture cosplay in Denmark in the mid-2010s in a transnational and 'productive fan' perspective. It is mainly informed by the state of the art of research in the mid-2010s.

For this purpose, *Cosplay* is divided into four parts. *Part One* introduces cosplay from the perspective of three Danish cosplayers and three Japanese cosplayers. The section is a revised and re-formatted version of the *Cosplayer! Manga Youth* exhibition which was translated into English by Jane Rowley. Photographs of exhibition displays and designs have been included where doing so fits the present purpose. Through nine sections the reader is introduced to Danish and Japanese cosplay, to the six featured cosplayers, cosplay photography, social spaces and the presence of fan immersion, crafts and creativity in the everyday life of cosplayers.

Part Two: Fan productivity and trans-Asian media referencing among Danish cosplayers presents the research in article format. Departing from the notion of inter-Asian mediated referencing, it identifies intimacies, distancing, reflexivities and performativities among a group of Danish productive fans in their consumption of and productive engagement with Japanese popular culture. The chapter thus argues that the Danish cosplayers constitute a confident, vibrant community, which sees itself in the midst of actualizing manga and Japanese media worlds against the backdrop of childhood and early youth literacies and intimacies. This 'actualization' and its productivity are largely disconnected from Japanese cosplay communities and Japan beyond the point of media cultures. In this context, the convergence of something identified as distinctively Japanese with something in which 'nationality' does not matter is a central part of the link between manga, anime, video games and cosplayer productivity in Denmark. The trans-Asian mediated referencing arguably is at its most lucid here, where the pursuit of national origins has all but collapsed.

Part Three: Interviews reproduces excerpts from interviews with Danish informants on childhood intimacies, feelings of belonging, cosplayer sociality, creative processes in idea development and dress making. This part aims to provide the reader a chance to explore key issues raised throughout the volume from the cosplayers' perspectives.

Part Four: Fan productions explores a central aspect of cosplay creative productivity, namely the making of cosplay costumes.

East Asian popular culture in a transnational perspective series

Cosplay is the first publication in the four volume series *East Asian popular culture in a transnational perspective: A National Museum of Denmark Collection*. This series explores issues around the consumption and appropriation of East Asian popular culture in a Danish context and asks what it can contribute to our understanding of cultural flows in an East/West perspective.

Volume One: Cosplay deals with a community of Danish fans of Japanese popular culture whose fandom makes them distinctly identifiable as productive fans; namely fans who *appropriate* characters, story-worlds and design from manga, anime and video games and who *produce* cosplay. It is argued that the Danish cosplayers constitute a confident, vibrant community, which sees itself in the midst of actualizing manga and Japanese media worlds against the backdrop of childhood and early youth literacies and intimacies. This 'actualization' and its productivity is largely disconnected from Japanese cosplay communities and Japan beyond the point of media culture. Further, the convergence of something identified as distinctively Japanese with something in which 'nationality' does not matter is a central part of the link between manga, anime and video games from Japan and cosplayer productivity in Denmark.

Volume Two: Hallyu deals with Danish fans of Korean popular culture. As consumers of Korean popular culture, not least K-pop (Korean pop music), these fans aspire to integrate into the Korean social fabric through career choice; they produce 'K-pop realities' by performing Korean dance, conforming to Korean aesthetics or beauty ideals, thinking through Korean story-worlds and finding viable alternatives to Danish youth sociality. This constitutes an example of how East Asian popular culture is present in the formation of Danish youth culture in the 2010s.

Volume Three: Purikura explores how an ethnographic exhibition in a Danish setting can enable playful productivity around East Asian popular culture, and, by extension, how this can become a step towards new ethnographic research and explorations. The book argues that mimetic empathy is one way to create understanding of and engagement in the ethnographic matter for visitors. The argument is based on a study of contemporary Japanese photo-booth photography (purikura) in its Japanese context and in the context of the National Museum of Denmark exhibition Girl with Parasol – Japan in the Photo Studio (2013-2014).

Volume Four: Museum Manhwa explores creativity at the interphase between cultural heritage institutions and creative industries. In 2019-2020, the National Museum of Denmark collaborated with four South Korean creators of comics and graphic art on themes related to Korea and Denmark. Choi Ho Chul, Ancco, Super Pink and Wooh Nayoung explored the Korean Collection in the National Museum of Denmark as well as themes related to Denmark historically and today. The volume presents the resulting comics and graphic works and their creation process in a 'museum fiction' and 'explorer' perspective. On this basis, Museum Manhwa examines in which ways objects, collections, narratives and expertise of museums and cultural heritage institutions can become a resource for creative industries in their work with narratives, characters, story-worlds, design, and aesthetics and how these creative collaborations can become integrated into the cultural heritage institutions, resulting in new types of content, work formats and visitor/user experiences.

In this manner, *Cosplay* (vol.1) and *Hallyu* (vol. 2) focus on Danish productive fans. They engage theories on 'Asia as method', 'inter-Asian mediated referencing' and 'Asian sensibilities' as the frame for an inquiry into transnational relations between East Asia and Denmark around flows of popular culture from the perspective of Danish 'productive fans'.

Meanwhile, *Purikura* (vol. 3) and *Museum Manhwa* (vol. 4) focus on the museum institution in a transnational perspective. They explore creativity and develop notions of playful productivity and museum fiction in a Danish cultural heritage and museum institution perspective.

The 'East Asian Popular Culture in a Transnational Perspective' series and the current volume on cosplay have been made with the academic as well as the general reader in mind. The general reader may find an easily accessible and extensive introduction to cosplay in Parts One, Three and Four of volume one.

I approach the topic from perspectives and fields such as fan studies, Japanese and East Asian studies and cultural studies. I strive to introduce relevant discourses and key terminologies in the research chapter (Part Two) in a manner which is accommodative towards students and scholars arriving from these various disciplines. While scholarly readers may only read the research chapter, the other sections will hopefully also be of value. Not only do the Parts Three and Four extensively present empirical findings, these sections may also inspire other scholarly approaches as well as provide a broad insight into cosplay in Denmark. In short, it is my hope that this book will serve its dual purpose as research publication and museum catalogue for the general and the scholarly reader alike.

Acknowledgements

First and foremost, I would like to thank all the Danish and Japanese cosplayers who kindly and with enthusiasm shared their interests, life-worlds and insights with me. In many cases they did this in interview sessions over a time span of several years. I would also like to thank each of them deeply for allowing me to publish their cosplay photos as well as photos of their costumes and props in this volume. I am also grateful to have had the oppotunity to collect some of the latter for the National Museum of Denmark.

The National Museum of Denmark is a cornerstone in the *East Asian Popular Culture in a Transnational Perspective* series. It has been a space for collaborative events and exhibitions with Danish fans of East Asian popular culture. In particular, I would like to thank each of the cosplayers, who made the cosplay exhibition, cosplay events and this book possible: Himo, Enilokin, Kelevar, Kurowko, Toshi, Hotaru, Marie, TinYasuo, Rose and Kami.

Several colleagues at the museum have been important in this regard. From the exhibition team behind *Cosplayer! Manga Youth*, I would like to express my warm thanks to Maruiska Solow, Bogdan Szymczyk, Kristine Møller Gårdhus, Amel Rahba, Stine Raun Nissen, Ieva Gardan, Michael Bjørn, Mikkel Hjorth Hansen and Christian Hede. Rikke Tjørnehøj has been an awesome work partner for most of these activities, always energetic, optimistic and supportive. Much the same words characterize Julie Emilie Stockholm Kragh and David Nicolas Christensen, who have also been engaged in these museum events and contributed immensely to developing ideas and connections. Christian Sune Pedersen has provided organizational support. Anna Frandsen, during her internship at the museum, made preliminary language revision and translation of parts of the volume, as well as offering valuable comments.

Martin Lindø Westergaard and Dorthe Møller with University Press of Southern Denmark have been excellent collabration partners in the production of this book.

Early stages of research for this book were enabled by a one-year grant from Kulturministeriets Forskningspulje. The publication of this book has been generously funded by Farumgaard-Fonden, Toyota-Fonden and the National Museum of Denmark. Thank you!

Last, but not least, I would like to thank my family and loved ones for their support and inspiration.

Cosplay Lexicon

Anime [アニメ]: Japanese term for animation and used globally to describe animation from Japan.

BlazBlue [ブレイブルー]: Japanese arcade fighting game from Arc System Works. Kurowko's favourite video game and cosplay.

Con [convention]: A large fair where fans share their interest in, for example, Japanese popular culture.

Cosplay [costume play]: In 1984, a Japanese filmmaker saw fans at an American Science Fiction convention dressed as sci-fi characters and called it コスプレ – *kosupure*, a word that can also be used for the cosplay costume.

Cosplay essentials: Used to describe everything cosplayers need for their costumes and performances.

Crossplay [cross-dressing cosplay]: A cosplayer with a character of the opposite gender or that plays with gender.

Dojinshi [同人誌]: Self-published materials, e.g. fan manga based on manga, anime and video games.

Enilokin: Nikoline's cosplay name - Nikoline spelled backwards.

Fan art: Artwork, e.g. an illustration, made by fans whose sources of inspiration include manga, anime and video games.

Fan fiction: Poems, short stories, novels, etc. created by fans based on an original work like *Harry Potter* or *Naruto*.

Fate [フェイト]: Started as a visual novel about the Holy Grail War developed by Type Moon. Toshi's cosplay.

Hetalia [ヘタリア]: Originally the Japanese web manga of Hidekaz Himaruya. Hotaru's cosplay.

Himo: Camilla's cosplay name, which means *hustler*. She was given the name as a joke, but it stuck.

Hotaru [蛍]: Directly translated means *firefly*. Hotaru only appears here under her cosplay name.

Kelevar: Julie's cosplay name from the (bad dog) Kelevra in the film *Lucky Number Slevin*.

Kurowko [クロコ]: Directly translated means *black child*, used for stage assistants in the theatre forms kabuki and bunraku. Kurowko only appears here under her cosplay name.

Manga [漫画]: The Japanese term for comics. Sometimes used more broadly to describe Japanese pop culture.

Photo shoot: A term from the world of fashion/advertising here used when a photographer takes a series of photos of one or more cosplayers.

Princess Tutu [プリンセスチュチュ]: Ballet-themed anime from Hal Film Maker Studio. Julie and Camilla's cosplay.

Purikura [プリクラ/print club]: A photo booth producing stickers, which emerged in Japan in the mid 1990s.

Rantaro the Ninja Boy [忍たま乱太郎]: Manga-based ninja anime from NHK (Japan Broadcasting Corporation). Hotaru's cosplay.

Saint Seiya [聖闘士星矢]: Originally a manga for boys about warriors protecting Athene. Hotaru's cosplay.

The Legend of Zelda [ゼルダの伝説]: Adventure/fantasy game series from Nintendo. Nikoline's cosplay.

Toshi [川平利光 / Toshimitsu Kawahira]: Short version of Toshimitsu. Toshi does not use a cosplay name.

Visual novel [ビジュアルノベル]: Interactive game with a stronger focus on visual narrative through static images and narration than player activity.

Yaoi [やおい]: Manga, anime, etc. that depict romance, love and sex between male characters. In Japanese discourse, yaoi commonly refers to the sexual variant.

Yuri [百合]: Manga, anime, etc. that depict romance, love and sex between female characters.

Part One:
Introducing Cosplay

Cosplay – costume play

Cosplay is the shortened form of costume play. Since the 1980s, young people in Japan have recreated characters from manga, anime and video games. With the global popularity of Japanese popular culture, costume play also went global and developed locally. Focus here is on how Japanese popular culture is created and recreated in Denmark and Japan. In what follows, you will meet three Danish and three Japanese cosplayers who transgress and play with the boundaries between fiction and reality, masculine and feminine, and Japanese and Danish. Six personal stories of fans as co-creators of the media world we all live in.

Japanese popular culture breaks boundaries

Since the 1990s, Danish children and young people have grown up in a media landscape where anime, manga and video games from Japan are as present as TV series and pop from the US and Denmark. Today, manga, anime and video games are the creative fuel which Danish and Japanese young people use to make their own characters, designs and stories as fan art, fan fiction and cosplay. Their fan products inspire young people worldwide – and the Japanese cultural industry.

Breaking Boundaries: A cosplay self-portrait

Hotaru has put on make-up and a wig, but not yet changed into a cosplay costume.
Is Hotaru a woman or a man?
Danish or Japanese? An artist or a fan?
A manga character or a real person?
Maybe it is not important.
Hotaru is ready.
Ready to enter the infinite universe of manga.

Introducing cosplayers

TOSHI / Hospitality and Good Manners

Many cosplayers push boundaries and cross borders. To Toshi from Tokyo, however, 'hospitality and good manners' is the motto for cosplay. He has worked in a cosplay event company for several years. Recently, he decided to become a cosplayer. He created the armour of the King Arthur character Saber from the manga, anime and light novel series *Fate/Prototype*. Saber has a strong sense of duty and justice. In Part One: Cosplay Stages (pp. 46-53), Toshi's perspective on the Japanese convention community is presented alongside photos of his cosplay activities in 2014 at the biggest fan, manga and cosplay convention in Japan, Comiket. You also can see his Saber cosplay in Part Four: Fan Productions (pp. 122-123).

HOTARU / Exploring the Dark Side

Hotaru is a cosplayer from Osaka, Japan. To Hotaru, cosplaying is mainly about perfecting a cinematic feel and exploring the dark side with images of violence and clashes between characters. She often transforms original story worlds and characters beyond recognition. With the Hetalia cosplay she strives to express themes and emotions like patriotism, comradeship and brotherly love between European male characters. Hotaru's explorations of Hetalia and other manga and anime universes can be found in Part One: Exploring the Dark Side (pp. 40-43). Her warrior (Saint Seiya) cosplay is documented in Part Four: Fan Productions (pp. 124-125).

KUROWKO / Love, Social Engagement and Purikura

Kurowko is a 24-year-old cosplayer from Osaka, Japan. She loves the characters Hazama and Terumi from the fighting game Blazblue. When she cosplays them, she becomes cool, strong, cute, attractive and mysterious - just like them. Kurowko shares these emotions locally and online. As Hazama and Terumi, she participates in charity and AIDS-awareness events at nursing homes, Santa runs, etc. In Part One: Purikura (pp. 44-45), you can see examples of Kurowko's purikura photos from her cosplay portfolio. Her original cosplay and self-made character Ko-rin is presented in Part Four: Fan Productions (pp. 126-127).

CAMILLA (HIMO) / Ridiculous Anime and Crazy Ideas

Camilla (Himo) is a 22-year-old Danish cosplayer. She meets up with Julie, Nikoline and the two other cosplayers Marie and Lea to watch anime. Even ridiculous anime inspires crazy ideas, which many hours of research, sketches, shopping for materials and sewing later become costumes, photo shoots and performances at conventions. In the interview excerpt in Part Three: The Anime Club (pp. 105-106), Camilla talks about the social life of watching anime. Her crossplay of Mytho from *Princess Tutu* is shown in Part Four: Fan Productions (pp. 128-129), and her selection of cosplay essentials for the cosplay exhibition is featured in Part One: Cosplay and Everyday Life (pp. 54-55).

JULIE (KELEVAR) / The Community Comes First

Julie (Kelevar) is a 21-year-old Danish cosplayer. She is active as a cosplayer, photographer and with the Danish magazine DKos (https://issuu.com/dkos). She is constantly exploring ways to 'translate' the stories, designs and characters of Japanese anime, manga and video games and American series into cosplay photos. To Julie, the social community of cosplay is key. In Part One: Photo shoot (pp. 32-39), you can read an interview on and see examples of Julie's photography and cosplay modelling. In Part Four: Fan Productions (pp. 128-129), you can see the Rue and Mytho cosplay from the Swan Lake-inspired ballet anime Princess Tutu, which Julie made with Camilla.

NIKOLINE (ENILOKIN) / Touching the Nostalgic Heart

Nikoline (Enilokin) is a 21-year-old Danish cosplayer and a big fan of Nintendo's Legend of Zelda game series, which she cosplays in photo shoots and at Danish and other European conventions. To Nikoline, cosplay is not only a Japanese universe of stories, characters and design. Disney's princesses also touch her 'nostalgic heart'. There is glitter in the air when Nikoline brings princesses to life with her needle and thread. You can see more of her designs and dreams about the Japanese 'badass' princess Zelda in Part Four: Fan Productions (pp. 130-131). This is further elaborated in an interview with Nikoline about costume making in Part Four: Nikoline on cosplay and costumes (pp. 132-144). Also, there are examples of how she, Camilla and Julie play with Japanese photo aesthetics in Part One: Purikura (p. 45).

Cosplay photography

TOSHI

"Cosplayers want to become someone else than who they are in real life. They think: 'If I can just be like my idol, or dress more sexually, or have a big sword.' They want to transform themselves and become almost *too* cute, handsome or strong. I think that's a big reason why they cosplay." (Photo p. 28)

HOTARU

"I know I risk negative reactions when it comes to exploring the darker side of history in a particular country through photography. So why do I choose these themes? It's like when you drink a lot of caffeine or go to a rock concert and get really excited. That's how I feel when I explore the dark side." (Photo p. 29 left)

KUROWKO

"I sometimes go to gaming arcades to play the *Blazblue* fighting game. In *Blazblue*, I love Hazama and Terumi. Everyone thinks these characters are cool and strong. But I also find them cute, attractive and mysterious. I put this love into my work with my Hazama and Terumi cosplay." (Photo p. 29 right)

HIMO / KELEVAR

Camilla

"I watch anime with my friends. We sit and laugh at how ridiculous they are. But then suddenly someone says: 'Hey, we could also do this ...' That starts a spiral that ends with us thinking: 'We've got to make it! This is way too epic for us five to be the only people who know about it'."

Julie

"Nobody really knows what cosplay is. They all want us to be the kind of kids that just want to dress up to escape real life. But most of us think: 'No, that's not what it's about. I'm fine with my life. I just enjoy dressing up'."

ENILOKIN

Nikoline

"*Anastasia*. I saw that film SO many times when I was a kid and thought: 'Wow, that dress is beautiful. I want to make it.' It's not important if my cosplay comes from a Japanese or an American series. What's important is whether I like the design and the character."

Photo shoot

High School of the Dead. The entrance to the basement of Hillerød Technical College, full of rubbish and dead leaves. "Try to look scared," Julie says to Kami in her Japanese school uniform. The world is being destroyed by a zombie invasion. Most of the pupils have already been infected – they are zombified and doomed. Kami can hear something coming, but where is it coming from? Now! Click.

During photo shoots, cosplayers recreate scenes or elaborate on characters, designs and stories from manga, anime and video games - improvising with their cosplay partners and the photographers. These photos are shared via social media and on-line communities like Facebook, Twitter, Cosplayers Archive, WorldCosplay and DKos.

Julie on being a cosplay photographer

"I do it because it's fun. I've been into photography longer than cosplay. It seemed natural to use my photography because so many models want pictures. You can make all kinds of scenes and stories in cosplay. So I use cosplay to improve my photography and editing skills. I usually do it with the models. I do everything myself. With natural light and no assistance."

Julie on photo shoot with Kami Renee

"We wanted something trashed – a dark atmosphere. She had to look scared because the zombies are about to get her. That's what we were aiming for. We also did some shots where she was more badass, pretending to shoot at the camera."

I'm Julie, I'm 21 and a cosplayer and photographer.

Julie on photo shoot with TinYasuo cosplay

"I tried to work with the direction of the light. It was the first time I used artificial lighting. I wanted to try some things out. Lighting from behind to create a halo around his hair, and from above. That divine feeling of him standing there and the world being a better place with God looking down on him. I also made it dark around him so he looks more alone – his pose is power crazed."

Julie on photo shoot with Nikoline (Enilokin)

"This was taken in Frederiksberg Gardens, Copenhagen. We mainly shot on the island with the Chinese teahouse. We started with pictures sitting by a tree, including some with her harp.

Then we went to find something else. We saw a pink bush and decided to take some pictures there. We took some portraits where both of us were in the bush so the branches and leaves create a fantastic pink veil.

We went to a place with a path where there were lots of trees that formed a dark tunnel."

Julie's own first cosplay

"It was around New Year 2011. It was just for fun, really. Me and two girls called Camilla, a photographer called Silas and Danny. We went to a location where there were walls of graffiti and took some pictures for fun."

Julie on Jack Vessalius cosplay

"I don't actually know the series. But my ex wanted me to cosplay Jack. I made my first version of him wearing a black suit. And I got hooked, so I made another version of him – the one in the photo with his classic, green jacket."

Julie on Red Queen cosplay

"I try to visualize the character. Take Red Queen. I see her as being elegant and regal, and evil too. Not like Disney characters where it's obvious they're evil, but a beautiful and together type. An actress once described how to walk like a queen. She said you put your shoulders back, your chest forward, and think 'murder' with your eyes. And that's what I tried to do when I was Red Queen - tried to think murder with my eyes."

Julie on self design of Calcifer cosplay

"It was difficult until I decided to make a 'self-design' of him where you design your own outfit [This character from *Howl's Moving Castle* is a ball of fire with eyes and a mouth]. I decided to make him into a woman. It was easier for me, but the design I had in mind also suited a woman better than a man."

Julie on Rue cosplay

"Camilla and I saw a video with Princess Tutu that made us want to make it. I only wanted to make this version of Rue next to me, because it just meant something to me. It's difficult to explain. It just appealed to me.

We wanted to perform, and we found out that the best story would include Kraehe. So we found a way to perform with both characters, and then I made both outfits. We tried some ballet poses, where we stand on our toes and make elegant movements with our arms. We also try to get inspiration from what ballet dancers do.

You could compare it to being in love. You get butterflies in your stomach and can't stop smiling. Something happens to girls when they put on a big dress. 'Oh, it's so fine and beautiful and ooh and aah'. There's just something about it."

Exploring the Dark Side – with Hotaru photo shoot

Saint Seiya (Knights of the Zodiac)

Nikoline had a blast cosplaying her childhood favorite movie *Anastasia* at the Paris Opera. Hotaru has followed *Saint Seiya* (*Knights of the Zodiac*) since kindergarten. While preparing the photo shoot, Hotaru worked closely with *Saint Seiya* design, characters and storyworld. The stories you grow up with can, in time, become the stories you tell. One of Hotaru's *Saint Seiya* armours is featured in Part Four: Fan Productions (pp. 124-125).

Rantaro the Ninja Boy (Nintama Rantaro)

Not only childhood stories, but also fan communities inspire cosplayers to find their own expressive forms. Growing up in the 1990s, Hotaru watched the NHK anime series *Nintama Rantaro* (*Rantaro the Ninja Boy*). The story is about a boy who joins a Ninja school. As the anime regained popularity in Japanese fan communities, Hotaru read some of the more serious *dojinshi* based on the series.

Rantaro the Ninja Boy (Nintama Rantaro)

The ninja cosplay photos were mainly taken in parks and forests in 2012 and 2013. The poses and visuals are not taken directly from anime or *dojinshi*. They represent an attempt to capture the bodily movements of ninja and make viewers feel the movement of the wind. Hotaru's ninja cosplay partner, Rikunosuke, has contributed to the harmony of the image.

Original cosplay

Hotaru creatively reworks anime, manga and fan-productions – often beyond recognition. But she also makes *original cosplay*. A cosplay is original when it is not taken from manga, anime or video games. This is a Yokai (ghosts and monsters, both good and evil) cosplay inspired by Japanese traditional folk tales. Hotaru explores the non-existent. The photo shoots take place in traditional houses.

Hetalia

Sometimes mainstream series are turned into violent, sexual fan universes. The globally popular anime and manga series *Hetalia* mainly deals with World War II. The characters are countries – mostly cute men. Many fans make dark, sometimes controversial *Hetalia* works. Hotaru does not intend her cosplay to be political. She explores the themes of brotherly love and hatred between European men during wartime.

Hotaru's *Hetalia* photos explore the darker side of historical events, patriotism and comradeship. Ideas are often developed online with her main *Hetalia* partner Nou, and from inspiration on location. History major Hotaru gets her inspiration from World War II documents, Western historical movies, martial arts scenes in Chinese movies and close studies of what she calls 'Aryan' and 'Latino' facial features.

Hetalia:
History of War / Photo: Dai
From left to right, rows 1 and 2: Italy, Germany, Japan
From left to right, rows 3 and 4: Ukraine, Russia, and Belarus

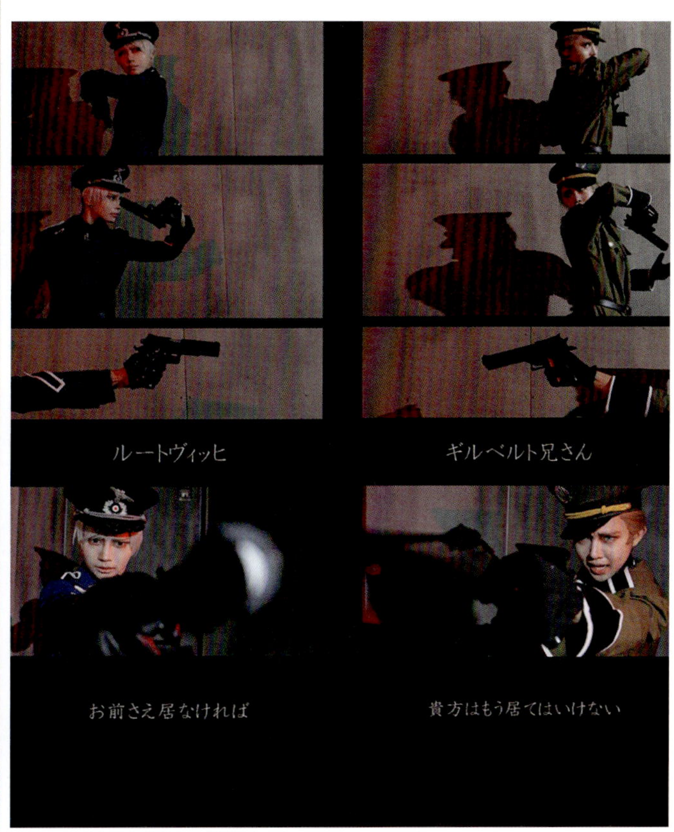

Hetalia:
Construction of the Wall / Photo: Dai
Prussia: "Ludwig. I have always wondered what would have happened if you did not exist."
Germany: "Brother. Your existence is beyond the time of history."

Purikura

Young Japanese people create visual stories about themselves digitally and on stickers in *purikura* – photo booths often located in gaming arcades. The photo booths perform a kind of digital plastic surgery based on Japanese ideals of female beauty. The eyes are made bigger, the skin lighter and smoother, the nose smaller and the head rounder. In Japan, cosplayers can use a *purikura* when they are at a convention or photo shoot. The National Museum of Denmark has on display a purikura named Heroine Face made by the Japanese company Furyu in 2012. Here are examples of purikura in Kurowko's cosplay portfolio and of purikura photo-stickers made by Julie, Camilla and Nikoline in Heroine Face. What happens when the *kawaii* (cute) style of the photo booth is mixed with the world of cosplay? For interviews with Julie, Camilla and Nikole on this fan productivity, see *Purikura* (Volume 3)

Kuruwko

Kuruwko

Julie & Camilla

Nikoline

Kuruwko

Nikoline

Cosplay stages

Convention

Cosplayers are performers who move between body and image and between the actual and the virtual. At fan conventions they meet other young people dressed as ninjas and Disney princesses, manga basketball stars and giant robots in a whirlwind of fan manga booths, video game zones and stalls with Japanese merchandise. They compete on stage and make new friends who cosplay the same series. In Denmark, J-Popcon and Genki are two of the main conventions featuring cosplay and Japanese popular culture.

Comiket

Comiket (Comic Market) is one of Japan's biggest, fan-run popular culture events. It was founded in 1975 and is held twice a year in Tokyo. The keyword is participation. Fans present and share their creations. This is also true of Danish conventions. But what are the differences? In *Japan/Denmark* below, Toshi and Marie express their participation-based perspectives on this.

In huge halls tens of thousands of fans sell their self-published manga (*dojinshi*) to around half a million visitors over three days. They are often funny, romantic, pornographic or artistic interpretations of popular manga, anime and video games.

In the outdoor areas of the Comiket, other productive fans – the cosplayers – bring characters from the same Japanese popular culture to life, posing for photographers and each other.

J-Popcon

ComiKet

Fan-made manga from Comiket 86 (Summer 2014). These are fan manga from *Hetalia*, *Saint Seiya* and *Rantarou the Ninja Boy*, which Hotaru cosplays, from *Blazblue*, which Kurowko cosplays, and *Fate/Prototype*, which Toshi cosplays.

Some of the books and CD-ROMs are erotic, many play with the action genre, and a few are genre experiments.

Cosplay photo albums and CD-ROMs from Comiket 86 (Summer 2014). These are albums with *Hetalia*, *Saint Seiya*, *Rantarou the Ninja Boy*, and many more. There are long queues for famous cosplayers, whereas other only sell a few copies.

Japan / Danmark

Every cosplayer has their own experience of and stories about conventions. The quotes and photos of Toshi below are from Comiket 86 (summer 2014). The world of the Japanese convention is juxtaposed with photographs from Danish conventions and quotes from Marie – one of the friends Camilla, Julie and Nikoline watch anime and has crazy cosplay ideas with.

The quotes reveal two different perspectives. It seems like a juxtaposition of Danish broadmindedness and Japanese formality. But is it really that simple?

Toshi

"My motto at the cosplay event I worked at was that 'cosplayers must always be polite.' But most cosplay events don't have that sense of hospitality, because most cosplayers are young. In my opinion, we have to have good manners. If young people learn that, and if they become good adults - good men and ladies - that's a good thing."

Marie

"At conventions there's something called *the anime dating game*. People dress up as characters that go on stage. The first character asks the other three characters – who she can't see – questions to choose who she wants to go on a date with. It's not usually a real date – it's about being in character. I remember one year one of the organizers said that if there was a male character on one side, there had to be female characters on the other. We were really offended by that. We were like: 'That's not a condition you can make. Especially not in this community'."

Toshi

"At Comiket and other cosplay events, fans don't care whether they are cosplaying a woman or a man. They feel comfortable and at ease being cross-dressers. But because ordinary people complain, some events only allow cross-dressing for women, not men. If a child sees a male crossdresser and asks its parents what it is, the parents can't explain it."

Marie

"A big part of being at a convention is that everyone is welcome. It doesn't matter who you are, what sexuality you have, or what colour your skin is. If someone on the cosplay scene says: 'I'm asexual,' everyone's fine with that. If you say it outside, I'd imagine people being more sceptical. And that I find interesting. Because it's neither Danish nor East Asian. It's something that emerges when the two cultures meet. The result is a really open space."

Toshi

“Being male or female makes a big difference in cosplay. One thing is that men don’t do make-up that well and can’t make a handsome enough face, because the male characters in the stories are too handsome, too strong and too smart. Plus the character style is very European. If we - including myself - wear those clothes, we feel awkward. That’s one of the reasons that there aren’t that many male cosplayers in Japan."

Marie

"In Denmark, we don't have the culture of *yaoi* and *yuri* they have in Japan. But because it's not a problem to talk about it, there's this meeting between Japanese content and Danish culture that creates a really special environment. The cosplay community in Denmark know what *yaoi* and *yuri* are, so it becomes more normal for people to be interested in the same gender, other genders or no gender in real life. Something happens in the mix that maybe doesn't belong to either Danish or Japanese culture."

Cosplay and everyday life

Cosplay and everyday life I

Camilla, Nikoline, Julie, Toshi, Kurowko and Hotaru make their own cosplay costumes, as do many Danish cosplayers. In Japan, it is more common to buy new or second-hand costumes on-line. Making a cosplay costume from scratch requires all kinds of materials bought on-line or in fabric and second-hand shops. Camilla is familiar with and thrifty in both worlds. She has selected most of the items displayed in the *Essentials* exhibition case shown here.

A cosplayer's room is almost inevitably filled to the brim with fabric remnants, wigs, shoes, sketches, design books, imitation weapons, etc. When Nikoline is working on her latest cosplay costume, her room becomes a dream factory.

Cosplay and everyday life II

Cosplays take up a lot of space. Many cosplayers keep them in cupboards, under the bed, in the attic or at their parents' house. Kurowko has to fold, squeeze and stack her Terumi and Hazama cosplays to get into her room. Hotaru's cosplays often get spattered with fake blood, dirt and sweat during photo shoots. These she throws away. To avoid bothering anyone, Toshi uses the balcony when he spray-paints his armour.

乙女ゲーム×少年マンガ
ドラマCD
「アルカナ・ファミリア」
2012.1.25 on sale
2012.3.28 on sale
1st EVENT
Pringles

Part Two: Fan Productivity and Trans-Asian Media Referencing Among Danish Cosplayers

Introduction

This chapter aims to critically examine what the study of consumption and appropriation of Japanese popular culture in a Danish context can contribute to our understanding of cultural flows in an East/West perspective. The chapter engages theories on 'Asia as method', 'inter-Asian mediated referencing' and 'Asian sensibilities' as the frame for an inquiry into transnational relations between Japan and Denmark centring on flows of popular culture as seen from the perspective of Danish 'productive fans'. [2] Concretely, it deals with a community of Danish fans of Japanese popular culture, whose fandom make them very visible as productive fans, namely fans who appropriate manga, anime and video games and who produce cosplay.

Cosplayers, as these productive fans are designated in global fan communities, mainstream media and within the Danish community, are commonly dedicated consumers of manga, anime and video games from Japan. They choose characters and to a certain degree story-worlds and designs from this Japanese mediascape as well as from the wider global fan universe. Based on this selection, cosplayers appropriate characters, often by making (sometimes buying) costumes, props, using make-up, wigs and lenses that

2 In *Hallyu* (2022) I examine this issue from the perspective of Korean popular culture.

render these characters in their own person. They mainly perform their characters on photo shoots, in convention halls, on stages and at walks. They share their photos online on diverse media platforms (YouTube, Facebook, WorldCosplay), exchange costumes, props, ideas, advice and information on upcoming events. While cosplay is often understood as intimately linked to Japanese popular culture, the emergence of cosplay is multilayered, national delimitations are contested and may be seen as intertwined with sci-fi and other fandoms with costuming. Suffice it here to say that this cultural praxis has long trajectories in both Japan and the US, and that cosplay gained popularity in Japan during the 1980s (Winge 2006).[3]

I have conducted fieldwork in the Danish cosplay community from November 2013 to June 2015.[4] The fieldwork combined semi-structured qualitative interviews with six predominantly female cosplayers in their early twenties and participant-observation of the Danish cosplay community. One key feature of the fieldwork was that a significant part of the interviews and participant-observations were conducted in the museum setting where I curated an exhibition and planned various outreach activities on cosplay in a Danish and transnational perspective.

From inter-Asian referencing to trans-Asian referencing: Danish productive fans

In the field of cultural studies, which examines intra-regional flows of culture, it has been argued that East Asia, in its linear trajectory of capitalist consumerist modernity (Chua 2008), more than being a historical condition

3 For an introduction to cosplay and cosplay photography, see Lamerichs (2013), Rauch & Bolton (2010), and Winge (2006).

4 The interview manual was put together and the project, in its current format, was initiated in October 2014.

significantly is also constituted and transformed by a trans-Asian public. This cultural geography is shaped by national and commercial interests, formed under influence of Western modernity and structural appropriation of not least American media systems in regional centres such as Hong Kong, Japan, and South Korea (Iwabuchi 2002; Chua 2012; Condry 2006). It is, however, also shaped by consumers, fans and grassroots communities, who establish affective communities of imaginative 'prosumers' (producer-consumers) and 'approreaders' (appropriator-readers) (Iwabuchi 2010b: 87). These terms constitute a focus on consumers as participants who not only passively receive and are ideologically formed by messages, but in the reception of cultural texts are appropriating and productive, and this often in counter-position to dominant understandings.[5] This terminology is imbued with aspirations, which often conflict with the commercial aspect of popular culture. A wide range of research has focused on trans-cultural pop cosmopolitans (Jung 2011), who establish themselves in on/off-line communities in the East Asian region around interests in, for example, films from Hong Kong (Chua 2012), manga, anime and video games from Japan (Iwabuchi 2002) or South Korean tv-dramas and pop music (Chua & Iwabuchi 2008; Kim 2013). These studies have complicated – and rightly so – the understanding of globalization as predominantly unfolding on a 'West to East' axis.

A key movement in this field is the advocacy for a regional re-orientation, termed 'Asia as method' (Chen 2010). Chen Kuan-Hsing argues that the notion of Asia may be used as an imaginary anchoring point, and that Asian societies can become one another's point of reference so that the understanding of self can be transformed and subjectivity rebuilt through decolonization, deimperialization and de-Cold War (ibid: 212). In this manner, claims Chen, the method can potentially highlight alternative understandings

5 An early, significant example of this frame in fan studies is Henry Jenkins' elaboration on 'textual poachers' (1992).

of world history. Ultimately, his project thus calls for a radical re-writing of global order and may be seen to imply a pan-Asianism.[6] Engaging the 'Asia as method' concept[7] with reference to affective communities of intra-regional, transnational pop cosmopolitans, Iwabuchi is a bit more cautious when he emphasizes a shift from 'mediated inter-Asian referencing' towards mutual collaboration on a grassroots level in the East Asian region.[8] Iwabuchi has elaborated on this notion in a range of papers (2010, 2010a, 2013, 2014, 2015), and explains mediated inter-Asian referencing as follows:

> People in Asian countries have long tended to face the West to interpret their own modern experiences, but the mediated encounter with other Asian modernities through the consumption of TV dramas, film and popular music from other parts of the region now offers people a wider repertoire for reflecting on their own lives and societies in the light of other East Asian modernities (2014: 51).

This modern East Asia should be understood as a 'loose cultural geography' (ibid: 48) imbued with regional cultural proximity and resonance, and the inter-Asian referencing as 'an integral part of people's mundane experiences of consuming media cultures' (ibid: 51). For instance, a Korean viewer of Japanese TV-dramas gains new understandings of herself, urban life, family matters and dating. Here, Iwabuchi shares common ground with Young Han Cho, who argues that consumption of pan-Asian pop cultures is limited to but not determined by this topography and enables East Asian sensibilities, which:

---

6 Chen does not use this term himself in *Asia as method.*

7 Iwabuchi also uses the term '(pop)Asia' as method in a 2012 Nippop seminar presentation from Bologna. https://www.youtube.com/watch?v=CkAo20raASs

8 Iwabuchi also uses the term to imply what should be expected of researchers in terms of academic theorization (Iwabuchi, 2014: 48). My employment of the term in this chapter does not have such implications.

> [f]ollowing Williams's insight [...] can be interpreted as emerging structures of feeling within the cultural geography of the region that encompass 'meanings and values as they are actively lived and felt' as well as 'a social experience which is still in process, often indeed not yet recognized as social but taken to be private, idiosyncratic, and even isolating' (p. 132) (Cho 2011:393).

Iwabuchi does not preclude inter-Asian referencing from social spaces beyond the loose cultural geography of East Asia. Notably, he has suggested that '[t]he inclusion of Asian migrants living in Western countries in a trans-Asian cultural connection would be imperative to go beyond a closed conception of "Asia" as a region (2015:7).

This Asian migrant consumption of East Asian popular culture in Europe and the US briefly touched upon by Iwabuchi has been pursued in various studies (Sung, 2013; Hübinette, 2012; Park, 2013). In *Hallyu* (2022), the second volume in this series, which examines Danish fans of Korean popular culture centering on a similar set of research questions as presented above, I argue that in some studies, the non-Asian viewers and audiences seem to be at least partially understood from the perspective of Western cultural hegemony. In a similar vein, Henry Jenkins' seminal fan studies (1992, 2006) disentangled the fan from dominant mainstream understandings as stigmatized, socially reclusive, excessive or even perverted, and launched the fan as a central figure for understanding identity formation in current participatory media cultures. Jenkins has demonstrated how top-down structures of media and contents industries and nation states intersect with fans, which in a wide range of ways appropriate and participate in popular culture and thus give shape to the convergence culture, which increasingly is characteristic of late modern, highly technological societies (Jenkins, Ford & Green, 2013) and which provides positionalities beyond that of soft power discourse. Despite this, Jenkins claims that the "pop cosmopolitan walks a thin line between dilettantism and connoisseurship, between orientalistic fantasies and a desire to honestly connect and understand an alien culture ..." (2006: 164). From this perspective, my study of a group of Danish fans of Korean popular culture and its interconnectedness with a reversal of transnational flows is worthy of note. It indicates the advent of Danish youth, who, to varying degrees of intensity and by dissimilar means, identify with and belong to the loose cultural geography of Korea. They aspire to integrate into the Korean social fabric through career choice, they produce K-pop realities by performing Korean dance, conform to Korean aesthetics or beauty ideals, think through Korean story-worlds and find viable alternatives to Danish youth sociality.

In conclusion, I am thus interested in seeing if we can further push the boundaries of this inter-Asian referencing. In the present volume, I explore this aspect from the perspective of Danish cosplayers, who are productively immersed in the consumption of East Asian popular cultures, and I suggest that the term 'trans-Asian mediated referencing' include also non-Asian productive fans. Beforehand, I outline the field of research on cosplay up to and around the first half of the 2010s.

Research on cosplay

In popular media, the transnational fan of Japanese popular culture is recurrently framed as the materialization and proof of the global attractiveness of Japanese popular culture and, is by extension, considered a fan from the perspective of Japanese soft power. In a critique of this, Brienza talks about an overheated rhetoric of invasion, conquest and revolution, and says that the discourse on soft power is more prescriptive than descriptive (Brienza 2014: 468). Most scholarship on the topic argues that the situation is much more complex, as here presented by Thomas Lamarre in a dialogue with Patrick Galbraith which question our understanding of *otaku*, a term which broadly refers to fans of Japanese popular culture:

> In sum, rather than a strict divide between ordinary fans and otaku, or between otaku consumers and corporate producers, there is a spectrum of productivity (368)... Even if we can identify territorial variations, the otaku mode is not entirely localizable, and thus entails a constant deterritorialization (Galbraith & Lamarre 2010: 370).

Likewise, studies on cosplay and cosplayers in the early 2010s are also mainly focused on the dynamic between cosplayers and local societies, and between the cosplay community and mainstream society, often from a gender or queer studies perspective. Frenchy Lunning thus examines cosplayers through the prism of 'abjected excess' and elaborates on the term as follows: "[c]osplayers do it [i.e. cosplay] because new subjectivities provide the pleasures and acceptance they lack in mainstream culture as abject subjects. It is therapeutic ... " (Lunning, 2011: 84). This marginalized positionality, which is a frequently visited trope in fan studies, invests energy in identifying subversion of the dominant meaning system (Ishikawa, 2010; Hellekson & Busse, 2014); not least female appropriations of male dominated commercial culture.

Joel Gn, in an attempt to get closer to the specificity of this social praxis, argues that cosplay is an "expression of emotional attachment to the animated body" (2011: 589), which somehow slips by and goes beyond the gendered body. Gn, discussing deviance and cosplay, argues for the limitation of a deviance that becomes bound up in a relation to a certain gender identity. Deviance, Gn argues with reference to R.C. Morris, 'based on agency, with its constant reference to established gender norms, precisely 're-inscribes' the dominant ideology it claims to work against ... ' (ibid: 250). Along the same lines, Nicolle Lamerichs approaches the issue of identity construction in an ongoing dialogue with Judith Butler's notion of performativity and drag.

Departing from Butler in her understanding of 'moments of degrounding or indeterminancy' (2011: 5.4), Lamerichs focuses on how cosplayers actualize both a narrative and their own identities. This leads her to thus argue that: "[c]osplay does not just fictionalize everyday life and give it an aesthetic dimension; it also shows how the fictional shapes the actual. Ultimately, cosplay is a vital example of how identity is constructed [...] It is through interaction with stories that we can imagine and perform ourselves" (ibid: 6.2).

Methodology

Informed by these approaches to inter/trans-Asian media referencing and to issues in cosplay studies such as fan productivity, abjection, emotional attachment to the animated body and performativity, fieldwork was carried out November 2013 to June 2015. It combined semi-structured qualitative interviews with participant-observation. The interview manual was developed around the research question regarding whether the Danish cosplay community can be identified as constituted by productive fans who, through trans-Asian mediated referencing and Asian sensibilities, are enabling an East Asiatization or loose cultural geography.

The semi-structured interviews were mainly conducted as continual sessions, mostly with individual cosplayers, in some cases with smaller groups. The participant-observations of the cosplay community were conducted in two distinct spaces:

1. Social fields where my informants constitute themselves in on/off-line social communities (for example in Facebook groups and online communities, and fan conventions). I also base my analysis on online observations on DeviantArt, in Facebook groups and through Danish cosplayers and cosplay photographers with individual artist profiles on Facebook.

2. The museum field in which informants were constituted as participants in museum activities and as exhibition collaborators.[9] Exhibitions include: 'Girl with Parasol' and 'Cosplayer!' Activities include: Opening days of 'Girl with Parasol', Cosplay evening event, 'NatNight' and cosplay photo shoot workshop.

Henry Jenkins along with other fan studies scholars has argued that the study of fan culture may be pursued from the position of the aca-fan (academic fan). I partially identify as an aca-fan in this study. An active consumer of East Asian popular culture myself, in an age perspective, as a social media-user and, partially, also in a gender perspective, I am positioned on the margins of and outside of the studied community. While the activation of the museum field does not compensate fully for this positionality, it served to establish a 'contact zone' (Pratt 2009; Clifford 1997; Petersen 2008, 2011) in which the relations to the informants were mutually activating. In other words, it construed a field for participant-observation in which the cosplayers were simultaneously engaged as co-producers of exhibitions and other museum activities. As curator and event (co)organizer, I arguably appropriated and produced exhibitions, activities and events in a manner not wholly dissimilar from the way in which my informants appropriated manga, anime and video games to produce cosplay. A central aspect of the participant-observations is thus that I activate a museum field. I have both a theoretical background and practical experience of operating within this field. I developed the theoretical basis for this field approach in connection with my PhD thesis and in later research in the format of methodological experiments with fieldwork in Korea, taking as my starting point the Korean collection in the National Museum of Denmark (Petersen 2008, 2011, 2015).

9 It is beyond the scope of this chapter to discuss the museum as an analytic field for cosplay. I elaborate on the topic in *Purikura* (forthcoming).

Recruitment of informants was conducted with the use of snowball sampling as method.[10] Informants / museum collaborators were thus recruited primarily through other informants, whether the point of entry was an interview or participation in museum activities. Recruitment in this way reflects these two distinct fields of participant-observation and the dynamic interaction between them. This has enabled me to understand how cosplayers reflected differently on their engagement in the same or similar activities, but, needless to say, may also have introduced bias in comparison with a methodology focused on representativity. Mainly, fieldwork has been structured around collaboration with four Danish cosplayers (Enilokin, Kelevar, Himo and Marie) in the preparation phase for the permanent theme exhibition 'Cosplayer – Manga Youth' and various outreach activities linked to the exhibition.[11] I first met Enilokin, Kelevar and Himo when they participated in a March 2013 cosplay event at the museum which was run in collaboration with the two cosplayers Rose and Kami, who were co-organizing that event and who were featured in the *Girl with Parasol* exhibition.[12] Later, I was introduced to Marie through them.

I initially did a semi-structured video-interview with Enilokin, Himo and Kelevar and individual semi-structured with each of them, followed by a wide range of planning meetings, e-mail communications and also a video-interview with each of them. I also contributed an article to a special edition of the Danish online cosplay magazine DKos for 'Cosplayer – Manga Youth', which Kelevar was editor of; in a way we thus reverse our roles. Apart from interviews and exhibition collaboration with Himo; Enilokin and Kelevar, I conducted research on the Danish (and also the Japanese) cosplay community in

10 In a Japanese context, this method is also used by Daisuke Okabe and Kimi Ishide in their studies of *fujoshi* (Okabe & Ishide 2012) and cosplayers (Okabe 2012).

11 https://en.natmus.dk/museums-and-palaces/the-national-museum-of-denmark/exhibitions/ethnographic-collection/cosplayer-manga-youth/

12 https://natmus.dk/museer-og-slotte/nationalmuseet/udstillinger/tidligere-udstillinger/pigen-og-parasollen/

a range of other ways.[13] I conducted a semi-structured interview with Marie and also assisted her, Himo and Kelevar on a video shoot in preparation for NCC (Nordic Cosplay Championship). I interviewed TinYasuo, whom I was introduced to by Rose and Kami and who also collaborated on two cosplay events at the museum. Apart from these informants, I have spoken to a range of cosplayers and photographers in the context of various museum activities.

Defining Danish cosplay

Before examining fan productivity as trans-Asian media referencing in Danish cosplay, I will outline the broader issues that characterize the Danish informants and their situatedness in the cosplay community in the mid-2010s.

The Danish cosplay community is young. The first J-Popcon convention, which is a main stage for cosplay in Denmark, was held in 2000 (with 200 attendants).[14] Since then, it has expanded in scale (3100 attendants in 2015).[15] The community is dynamic, very active online and undergoing constant changes as to the means of communication and presentation formats. The time of my fieldwork marked the transition phase from DeviantArt to Facebook as the main platform for interaction with other cosplayers and, in particular, of self-presentation.[16] Interactivity, searchability and avoidance of 'spam'[17] were all mentioned as reasons for this migration. Perhaps more than anything, Facebook is an SNN which congenially puts the individual at the forefront, an issue I will return to shortly. The Danish cosplay community also congregated on

13 I worked closely with three Japanese cosplayers, Hotaru, Kurowko and Toshi, for the cosplay exhibition and related events (see Parts One, Three and Four). In preparation for the exhibition, I had a wide range of communications, meetings and interview sessions with them.

14 http://www.j-popcon.dk/da/pages/129-om-j-popcon

15 On the J-popcon website, 2007 is mentioned as a milestone. This year was the first with qualification for World Cosplay Summit in Nagoya, Japan.

16 TinYasuo, Himo, Enilokin, Kelevar, MieRose and Kami all have artist pages on Facebook.

17 For instance, one informant exemplified 'spam' as pornography uploaded under the pretext of being cosplay photography.

Facebook around groups such as *Cosplay i Danmark* [Cosplay in Denmark], *Cosplay Køb, Salg, Bytte* [Cosplay Buy, Sell, Exchange], *Cosplay hjælp, tips og tricks!* [Cosplay help, tips, tricks!], *Cosplay Crafting, Alt fra J-pop kulturen* [Everything J-pop culture] *J-popcon, Genki, Dkos.*

Informants who participate in the study were actively participating in international (mainly European) conventions, competing on stages and also frequently doing photo shoots in collaboration with highly experienced cosplay photographers. Age- and experience-wise, these features set them apart from the majority of cosplayers in the community. In their early to mid-20s, they characterized themselves as belonging to the older generation.

Social composition

Main conventions focusing on Japanese popular culture and with cosplay activities are J-Popcon, Genki SVS Con, Geekcore, Hydracon and KoyoCon. These annual conventions are key off-line social spaces of Danish cosplay. Apart from that, there are various other conventions with cosplay activities; Copenhagen Games, Copenhagen Comics, DR Spil, etc. With regards to conventions there are several distinct subgroups and distinctive activities within the larger convention community, as here related by TinYasuo:

> It is grouped, but that's what makes it so nice. That's exactly why I think it is so ideal ... cosplay is more than one hobby ... it is grouped in the manner that we have the 13 to 15-years-old and around that age, who not really felt that they belong. And who like to fool around, shout and yell and such, and enjoy that. And there's room for that ... Then there are those who simply participate. They buy a costume and join the con where they hang out with other people, who are also there just to have a good time. Perhaps they are not that much into what the costume should look like; they are there for the social aspect ... Then there are the gamers, they are there just to enjoy gaming. They go into the game room and maybe the dealer room. There is also room for them. And

> yet again there are some who are a bit more into it [cosplay], well they perform, but maybe not at the major competitions, but they do perform and they are doing stuff here and there. They are there, too. Then there are those who come just to do photo shoots, and then there are those who are totally into the costume aspect … and therefore there is this thing that you can always find somewhere, where you belong in one way or another (TinYasuo, interview)

While generally, the overall communal spirit and its diversity is highly praised by cosplayers, it is also a potential source of friction. A recurrent negative example I heard of was the occasional fans, who were oblivious of or ignored (un)written rules of bodily contact, and treated other cosplayers as if they were in fact the character.[18]

Abjected subjectivities

This strong sense of community arguably exists alongside an equally strong sense of individuality. Among Danish cosplayers, individualism and competitiveness are discursively construed as being productive, constituent elements in the development of community. This leads to a peer sociality of best practice. In some cases, it leads to idolization. This peer sociality has been explored by Ito Mizuko in a study of the anime-related fan subbing scene. Ito argues that young participants "learn from more experienced peers, who share their passionate and specialized interests (Ito et al. 2009). This kind of learning and skills development is highly motivating and tied to a sense of autonomy and self-actualization" (Ito 2012: 194). Interestingly, a role player informant, who made a small, informal survey among her roleplaying

18 There may also be other sources of conflict within cosplay. When preparing for the cosplay exhibition at the National Museum of Denmark, I was requested not to feature the most 'renowned' Danish cosplayers as this potentially would elicit some negative response caused by the fact that the same cosplayers always get all the attention. In another related example of friction, some Danish cosplayers were the objects of anonymous criticism on the imageboard website 4Chan.

friends, said that some respondents regarded the cosplayers as narcissists. Some K-pop fan informants considered participants in the cosplay community to be quite extrovert in comparison with their own community (see further, Hallyu (vol. 2) 2022).

These aspects, however, do not entirely discount the notion of abjection and marginalized subjectivities widely featured in fan research. One informant thus suggested that 90% of cosplayers have a past that includes being marginalized or bullied. The issue of accuracy of this informal statistics aside, this narrative of being different and of turning this disadvantageous difference into collective creativity was a recurrent plot in cosplayer narratives. This discourse fits nicely into Lunning's theory of abjection and Gn's notion of deviance mentioned above.

Various kinds of friction between the cosplay community and mainstream society also came up during conversations: Kelevar expressed it thus: "Nobody really knows what cosplay is. They all want us to be the kind of kids that just want to dress up and escape real life. But most of us think: 'No, that's not what it's about. I'm fine with my life. I just enjoy dressing up.'" In particular, an article in the Danish major newspaper *Politiken*, which featured J-Popcon 2014, was widely regarded in the cosplay community as an example of mass-media misrepresenting the Danish cosplay community. Parents were also considered by some cosplayers as people who really do not know what cosplay is. As Enilokin inferred, however, in Denmark, they had to come to terms with and accept this. One cosplayer referred to an uncomfortable conversation she had with an elderly male teacher at her college. He was overtly focused on what he considered to be the fetishist, sexual drive behind (her) cosplay. In Japan, this sexualisation is a recurrent mainstream critique and fascination,[19] cosplay being a creative space of youth experimentation,

19 See for example Okabe (2012).

but sexual deviance is also a minor theme in Danish discourse. There is also an awareness among the cosplayers that cosplay may be construed as hyper-sexualized by outside observers for a reason. One informant remarked that many of the younger cosplayers post 'stuff', which they may end up regretting and mentioned an early personal experience of posting a cosplay video, which ended up on an Asian gay porn site. Generally, however, most Danish cosplayers were quite confident about their hobby and predominantly spoke of positive interactions with non-cosplayers – something they compared favourably to the situation for Japanese cosplayers, who they assumed lived with the duality of being more widely recognized by mainstream society but at the same time also facing media and mainstream criticism – an assumption I also found reflected in my conversations with Japanese cosplayer informants, who occasionally brought out this matter.

Fan productivity as trans-Asian media referencing in Danish cosplay

Having now set the stage, I will examine how Japan figures in the lives of the Danish cosplayers through four themes: childhood media intimacies and adult fan productivity, Japan and Japanese media worlds in the Danish cosplay community, creativity and transcendence in communal spaces, and bodies as 'stateless' (*mukokuseki*). Arguably, childhood and early youth experience with Japanese media cultures is key to the exploration of fan productivity and trans-Asia referencing in the Danish cosplay community, and I therefore begin with this aspect.

Childhood media intimacies and adult fan productivity

Japanese media cultures as childhood discovery and nostalgia is a motif that runs through the interviews with most cosplayers. Some relate of formative experiences of discovering manga, anime and video games from Japan in their childhood. This creates an intimacy, which can manifest itself in many ways, but strong and lasting attachments to certain story worlds and characters is one recurrent narrative. TinYasuo is one such poignant example of how childhood media consumption may shape a particular form of intimacy with and literacy in Japanese media universes, which becomes the backdrop for adult fan productivity. TinYasuo discovered and engaged in this through the consumption of *Pokemon* and *Dragon Ball* around the age of six and then transferred this experience into doing manga-inspired drawings. He accentuated the important role this consistent media consumption had in his early development of literacy. The intimacy and familiarity with 'things Japanese' was thus already internalized through a repertoire of aesthetics and narrative sensibilities from childhood. Not all things were linked to Japanese popular culture. TinYasuo also mentioned how sewing and acting were activities he became familiar with early on. This points towards an assembly of competences and interests, which would later come together and form the backdrop for his engagement in cosplay.

In the late 1990s, *Pokemon* and *Dragon Ball* were widely accessible through TV-channels, bookstores and public libraries in Denmark. It must thus be considered mainstream consumption among Danish kids at the time and not something which in itself distinguishes the fan from other consumers or cosplayers from non-cosplayers. The particular set of interests, competences and possibly the intensity of his consumption, however, set TinYasuo apart from his classmates. He spoke of being an outsider and how he experienced this status as partially interrelated with his 'manga intimacies'. Interestingly, though, in his account, these same skills also contributed to gaining respect among peers as his drawing skills gradually evolved.

This encounter with manga and anime in childhood has a double effect. Japanese cultural products enter a canon of cultural products and become mythologized as nostalgia. Concretely, cosplayers re-activate this nostalgia by performing often grown-up versions of childhood media experiences; Burlesque Disney, for example. Certain Japanese media products thus have become 'naturalized'. At least on a superficial level this is an East Asian sensibility and trans-Asian mediated referencing. To these Danish consumers, the encounter with these media universes is not different from the encounter with American or Danish media universes. As a case in point, Enilokin designated the emotional experience of revisiting childhood media as a grown-up productive fan as being hit 'right in the nostalgic heart!' Enilokin highlighted certain traits that are common for the characters which she explores through cosplay – in disregard of whether these are American or Japanese; they are feminine characters who combine cuteness with a fighting spirit, whether that be Anastasia (*Anastasia*) from Fox Animation Studios, Zelda (*Legend of Zelda*) from Nintendo or characters from *Sailor Moon* (Kodansha; Toei Animation).

The question of course is whether the fact that a few manga, anime and video games spill into the broader cultural geography dominated by US, Danish and European cultural products is sufficient to allow us to speak of an Asian sensibility in Denmark. To begin with, research on Japanese media and popular culture points towards the fact that consumption of many Japanese products in Europe and the US is not a deliberate engagement with 'something' Japanese. Often, the Japanese origins are irrelevant to the consumer and even deliberately obscured by producer and distributor (Ruh, 2014). In the context of the creation of anime and computer games, Iwabuchi elaborated on the feature of non-Japaneseness in *Recentering Globalization* (2002). Here, he explains it as follows:

> The characters of Japanese animation and computer games for the most part do not look "Japanese". Such non-Japaneseness is called *mukokuseki*, literally meaning "something or someone lacking any nationality," but also implying the erasure of racial or ethnic characteristics or a context which does not imprint a particular culture or country with these features (28).

As we have just seen, American media products seamlessly fit into the cultural platform of cosplay in Denmark. Many Danish cosplayers perform characters, without always and necessarily putting any emphasis on whether these are taken from Japanese or American mediascapes. In fact, the activity of cosplay itself, while mostly discursively formed as part of an ensemble of Japanese popular culture, as seen above, is not unconditionally linked to Japan by Danish cosplayers. As stated by Enilokin: "[Cosplay] comes from all over. It probably started in the US or something like that", and Kelevar: "To me, it is not important that my cosplay is from a Japanese series, but Japan interests me."

Further, my research did not indicate a universal narrative of trans-Asian mediated referencing or East Asian sensibilities acquired through childhood consumption. Some cosplayers would indeed make clear that as media consumers and cosplayers they had a preference for Japanese manga, anime and video games, and that they found the US comic style/superhero genre to be unrefined. However, as is clear at Danish cosplay conventions, in the editorial line of the Danish cosplay magazine DKos[20] and in my qualitative interviews with informants, this is far from a universal narrative in the Danish cosplay community. In fact, most cosplayers I interviewed also cosplayed from European (web comics, radio show) and in particular American (Disney, D.C., Marvel etc.) series and media universes. The case of TinYasuo, who we

20 The DKos volumes One through Nine have the following caption: 'Photo shoots with both Western and Eastern series' on the front page.

saw attain literacy through manga, exemplifies one path into cosplay and one path from consumption to fan productivity, and that of Enilokin who was recurrently 'hit right in the nostalgic heart' by both American and Japanese cultural products is another. All cosplayers I interviewed, however, discovered cosplay by way of manga and anime. In some cases, there was merely one year between the discovery of manga and anime and then becoming involved in cosplay. The Danish cosplayers I interviewed had cosplay-like formative experiences in the form of dressing up as Japanese characters on their last day of school and for Shrovetide ('fastelavn'). While most cosplayers distinguish themselves from such widespread Danish costuming practices, which is one recurrent mainstream perception of cosplay ('all year Shrovetide'), these experiences at least to some degree formed an early backdrop. This discovery of Japanese media culture came about through a range of sources, such as watching television, through friends and family members and at the local library. Google searches would lead them on to predominantly Western fan works, such as fan art, fan fiction, Anime Music Videos and cosplay photography. This gradually acquired media literacy makes up for the almost transcendental experience of coming to a convention for the first time and to here recognize the characters being cosplayed. It is mediated referencing at its most mundane, but also at its most powerful. Interestingly, this experience was also mentioned by a role player informant as the thing that made her feel alienated at cosplay conventions. She simply lacked the Japanese popular culture references. K-pop fan informants, however, spoke of the wow effect of coming to a convention despite lacking the references.

While intimacies, media literacy and fluency certainly link the early consumption of manga, anime and video games to the fan productivity of cosplay and constitutes one path of entry, this link could be overstated. Some informants descibed how they were too busy with cosplay activities, college, work and everyday life to keep updated on the anime, manga and video games scene. While keeping Joel Gn's notion of 'emotional attachment to the animated body' in mind, this observation urges us to reconsider the relation between cosplayers and the specific characters and story-worlds, they cosplay from. Also, it urges us to view the trans-Asian referencing in a more diffuse, distributed perspective. In other words, the 'original' Japanese media productions (manga, anime, video games) is but one point of reference and inspiration. For example, and closely related to the peer sociality aspect, we also find mature and experienced cosplayers on Facebook and other media, and their productivity is consumed (even deified) by the younger generation and peers. Arguably, thus, the 'older', stage-performing cosplayers are consumed in a manner that cannot easily be distinguished from the consumption of Japanese media products with popular characters, and they also inspire cosplayers in their choice of characters. In this way, there is an intersection of intimacies and detachment, distance and closeness to Japanese media culture.[21]

Further, having a kind of attachment to or affection for a certain character, whether, as we have seen, this is through anime or via other cosplayers, certainly does not exhaust possibilities. A costume or fan art can be a starting point, and then this aesthetic attachment may lead to fannish engagement with manga and anime. Notably, an interest in cosplay and Japanese popular culture is also an entry point to a larger range of fandoms. Several fans of Korean popular culture, whom I interviewed, discovered this field by way of an interest for Japanese popular culture.[22]

---

21 Younger cosplayers at cons and/or Facebook followers are sometimes regarded and addressed as fans, a circumstance which imbues more experienced, stage-performing cosplayers with an obligation to do their best and to consider how to communicate not least on social media.

22 A case in point, Marie related that she was reading Teen Wolf fan fiction, but that this would not have come about if she had not started reading fan fiction as part of her engagement with Naruto and cosplay.

While an engagement with Japanese media cultures can open up for a plethora of engagements with other seemingly unrelated media cultures, media discovery in this way has Japanese media cultures as constitutive of orientation and taste, at least in the case of Danish Hallyu (Korean wave) fandom. This strengthens the argument for the emergence of trans-Asian referencing as constitutive of a loose cultural geography in certain Danish on/off-line social spaces. The multidirectional referencing and orientation may be negatively construed by those fans who idealize cosplay as an expression of fandom focusing on the 'original' characters and series,[23] but it nevertheless shows how fluid and open boundaries between media industry and fans are in terms of productivity and consumption.

In extension, this spectrum of productivity (as we have seen it explained by Lamarre above) is reminiscent of Iwabuchi's observations on consumption in Asia.

> People no longer consume "the West" or a "Westernized Asia" but an "indigenized (Asianized) West"; they are fascinated neither with "originality" nor with "tradition," but are actively constructing their own images and meanings at the receiving end (2002: 105).

Danish cosplay, in its relation to Japan, is unfolding in a spectrum between consuming Japan and consuming through cosplayer productivity an indigenized (Westernized) Japan. Notably, the same cosplayer can easily traverse up and down this scale, and it is precisely in this scaling that we should pursue the notion of trans-Asian mediated referencing.

---

23 At a J-Popcon workshop on fandom, a German event organizer described how some German cosplayers 'examined' peer cosplayers in order to scrutinize the level of their knowledge of the characters they were cosplaying.

Japan and Japanese media worlds

Cosplay, as now established, is a cultural field which has Japanese media cultures as its key constituent element and which arguably constitutes a loose cultural geography. This, however, does not automatically translate into inter-personal communication and interaction with Japanese cosplayers and fans, which, as already seen, is Iwabuchi's idealistic notion of mutual collaboration on a grassroots level. The connection between Danish and Japanese cosplay and cosplayers is much less structured and intense, and in terms of the level of engagement and familiarity in the Danish cosplay community, it does not in any way match manga, anime and video games.[24]

Considering the fact that the Danish cosplayers to differing degrees were immersed in and well-informed on Japanese media cultures, while Japanese cosplay and cosplayers were distant,[25] it is quite interesting that not only language but also cultural differences were mentioned as barriers to Japanese cosplay by the Danish informants. Firstly, we should consider the more idealistic or prescriptive aspect of 'Asia as method', where Iwabuchi speaks of people's mediated dialogue, the potential for mustering a progressive transnational imagination and mutual collaboration on a grassroots level. At the transnational, inter-personal level, it is not possible on the basis of my study to identify a progressive social space, which is constituted by Japanese

---

24 Thus, for example, the reference to Japanese cosplay was often made through Reika, an internationally renowned Japanese cosplayer, who visited J-Popcon in 2014 as judge and special guest. Also, Danish cosplayers are generally speaking quite confident about the state of Danish cosplay in terms of individual creativity in making costumes and photography. In some cases, this confidence was stated through comparison with Japanese tendencies to buy cosplay costumes, to do heavy photo shopping, its preference for the doll-like and lack of realism. Having experienced Japanese cosplay photography through fieldwork in Tokyo and Osaka, such statements surprised me somewhat. Japanese cosplay photography has impressed me with its diversity, its often creative employment of the art of photo shopping and realism.

25 Danish cosplayers often mentioned the U.S as a more commercialized setting than the Danish, and while interested in such aspects, they also gave various examples of how this fame culture had negative downside in terms of anonymous haters and rants on image board websites. As participants and competitors, some had experiences with Japan but were mainly much more familiar with the European community (Sweden, Germany, France and England).

and Danish cosplay communities.[26] Iwabuchi also remains skeptical about how such mutual collaboration can in fact emerge from this parallel consumption of media products in Asia. However, there are social spaces where Danish cosplayers come into direct contact with Japanese cosplay and cosplayers: Some Danish cosplayers travel to Japan, there are international cosplay social media where Western and Asian cosplayers congregate and the Japanese cosplay community also organizes conventions with an international focus.

TinYasuo along with his cosplay partner, Shinji, had firsthand experience with the Japanese cosplay commmunity. At the Danish main scene for cosplay competitions, J-Popcon in 2014, the two qualified for the World Cosplay Summit (WCS) in Nagoya, Japan. TinYasuo's description of his encounter with Japan and the Japanese cosplay community in the context of the WCS mainly focused on interaction with other national representatives from abroad and on finding ways to accommodate to Japanese fans attending the various events. Concretely, for example, by cosplaying the hugely popular Lewi from *Attack on Titan* and being acceptant of and playing along with the understanding that Japanese fans approached him as *the* character. This sensibility, no doubt, is linked to TinYasuo's media intimacies and childhood literacy, as already mentioned. As retold, the identification with Japanese cosplay was thus predicated on the activation of a different set of cultural codes around how fans approach cosplay and cosplayers, rather than intimacy per se. This no doubt has a lot to do with his experiencing Japanese cosplay through the lens of a foreign national representative and idol in the WCS setting. Another part of TinYasuo's narrative, however, manifested itself as a

---

26 Japanese cosplayers I interviewed explained this as the outcome of the closed character of the Japanese cosplay community. One Japanese cosplayer I spoke with was critical of how Japanese conventions were not geared towards participation from global fandoms. They inferred that, while there may be intra-community competition and even hostility, the Japanese cosplay community was seen as a safe space. In the museum field, the three Japanese cosplayers who visited the museum for cosplay events and seminar swiftly 'connected', exchanged ideas for cosplay and made collaborations beyond the museum space.

sense of belonging, even coming home. As a cosplayer, he temporally *became* Lewi to Japanese fans. 'In civil', travelling through Japan after the WCS, he experienced being received and treated as *Ikemen* (cool, good-looking guy). TinYasuo was in other words identified as a male beauty. In her study of the Singaporean fandom of male K-pop stars, Sun Jung (2011) has traced the trajectory of the male beauty in the cultural geography of East Asia back to manga aesthetics and sensibilities.

In TinYasuo's own words:

> Culturally, I really felt at home although I grew up in another culture. But I have been interested in this for so long, and all of a sudden I was not seen as the tiny, feminine guy. I fit in with my height and size. It was just like: 'People here think I am hot. What's that all about?' (TinYasuo, interview)

This experience of being foreign, yet part of the cultural geography, is explained as a confluence of clothing style, physiognomy and familiarity with Japanese concepts of attractiveness. Apart from being a recount of youth travel experience, it speaks of mutually relatable energies nestled in trans-Asian referentiality and its dormant potentialities. Whether the evocation and appreciation of Japanese notions of attractive masculinities is the kind of progressive transnational imagination Iwabuchi is aiming for is another matter, of course.

Creativity and transcendence in communal spaces

As has now been argued, Japan (beyond manga, anime and video games) and Japanese cosplay is not per se an object of fandom, or necessarily something familiar, intimate and relatable among my informants. Cosplay in Denmark is better described as a social space around friendships and activities; a predominantly Danish and inter-European community loosely organized and constituted around conventions and diverse Danish and English-language social media in which Japan, Japanese media and popular cultures figure prominently. Next, I will examine two social spaces, namely communal media consumption and the convention in order to explore this configuration.

An example of communal media consumption is the 'anime club'[27] in which four cosplay informants (Enilokin, Kelevar, Himo and Marie) participated. Here are excerpts of how they spoke of this recurrent activity in individual interview sessions:

> It is really just to enjoy it, like when you have a movie night. We have simply chosen to do it with anime, because that's what we are having fun with. We laugh a lot and find loads of series, which we wouldn't be watching if it wasn't because we watched them together (Kelevar, interview).
>
> We mostly watch them for their entertainment value; stuff which is plainly silly or just really, really strange. And part of it, I would say, is to get to sit there and criticize (Marie, interview).
>
> I haven't seen an anime by myself in years. To me, it's something social. Those anime we watch are a bit ridiculous. It's something about us making fun of just how bad they are. And then suddenly it's there: "Actually, you could do something like this [as cosplay]..." and then it's opened up, and we all join in. It's like a spiral and it just goes on and gets bigger and bigger. At the end we are thinking: "We just have to do this [cosplay together at a convention]! It's way too epic for just the five of us to know about it [...]The spur of the moment. That social thing. That's just my type of cosplay. That's why I do it. (Himo, interview).[28]

27 My informants did not have a name for this activity as such, but named it 'anime club' as shorthand when talking about it to me. I follow their praxis here.

28 There was a fifth participant in the anime club who I did not interview.

The anime club is an event in which these five friends engage as critical, perhaps even slightly condescending, spectators in search for a fun, carefree time together, but, as mentioned by Himo, they end up getting carried away, overwhelmed and collectively spurred to fan productivity. This productive eruption could possibly take place around anything. The combination of shared media preferences among these friends, and the 'ridiculous' storylines, visual excellence and goofy humor of the anime they watch, however, facilitate a collective creative eruption at the intersection between identification and distancing. Chua notes how, in the intra-Asian context, the watching of imported TV-series is an intermittent process of identification and distancing (2008: 84). Further elaborating on this, Cho speaks of regional resonances in terms of an uneven but simultaneous temporality. He regionalizes this familiarity as partially related to Confucianism (2011). The five cosplayers' communal experience cannot be characterized as intra-regional resonance; much less as being impacted by Confucian contents.[29] We have seen how TinYasuo experienced this confluence of identification and distancing during his visit to Japan. It underpins a boisterous contagiousness, which, as explained by Himo, just has to be shared with the broader Danish cosplay community. Himo mentioned the "swimming anime" *Free!*, which the friends watched and soon did a group cosplay of (in a slightly changed line-up) crossplaying five of the male high school swimmers from the anime at J-Popcon.

The social setting of the anime club and its productivity is reminiscent of *matsuri* as discussed by Patrick W. Galbraith and Thomas Lamarre in their engagement with the *otaku* term in its Japanese context. Galbraith infers that "[t]he idea of consumption as an event is in keeping with otaku de-

29 The significance of Confucianism as a constitutive element of the loose cultural geography of East Asia is debatable and indeed debated. Further, Chua (2008) and Cho (2011) speak of TV-series, not anime.

scriptions of their activities in terms of *matsuri*, or "festival." Many otaku use *matsuri* to describe the group dynamic that forms around special events ..." (Galbraith and Lamarre, 2010: 365). None of the Danish cosplayers referenced any specific Japanese mode of consumption as related to their sociality and fan productivity.I am not implying that this kind of sociality around anime is something inherently, essentially Japanese. Still, there is a valid point in considering the intentionality of anime creators and the industry (Condry, 2013) and its potential effects when approaching the productivity of the Danish anime club.[30] In other words, it is worth considering the ways in which anime, for example, is created with an implicit understanding of how fans interact with it. The *matsuri* term is thus relevant in the sense that the social creativities that are unleashed in the encounter with 'ridiculous' anime are channeled into a specific set of fan productivity, such as costume-making practices and later performativity in a convention setting, which we will consider next.

Marie, while talking about the Danish convention community, brings us one step closer to understanding the particulars of how the communal consumption of the swimming anime *Free*, with its focus on *ikemen* in swimsuits, turns into five female friends performing crossplay. During an interview, Marie mused how in Denmark there is a great deal of openness in the cosplay community and at conventions with regard to physical intimacy (holding hands, skinship, etc.) as well as being openly acceptant of a variety of sexualities, including a-sexuality. The turning point in the narrative came when Marie said that she first thought that the specificity of this type of intimacy and openness was a perfectly common part of Danish youth sociality, but upon reflection came to realize that it is something specific to the cosplay community.[31]

30 In a comparative perspective, this point would have to be pursued further through fieldwork and interviews with Japanese cosplayers watching anime together.

31 This physicality would have to be compared to other social spaces of Danish youth communities, at open-air music festivals, for example. An interview with an informant from the Danish roleplaying community indicated the existence of a similar phenomenon in her community.

> I think to some extent this acceptance comes from ... I mean, the whole thing with *yaoi*, it comes from East Asia, for example. But in Denmark it's not an issue to talk about it [varieties of sexuality]. Yet it might be difficult to talk about it in East Asia. It's not something you walk around telling people. Whereas it's not an issue here [in Denmark]. We just don't have it [*yaoi*]. And I think it relates to the fact that we are able to talk about it and we don't have it [*yaoi*]. Then all of a sudden it becomes this total acceptance [openness], because everyone [in the cosplay community] knows what it is and then it becomes more normal that real people also can be into the same gender or others genders or no gender. But it's an idea (Marie, interview).

Yaoi is a genre term, which is partly identical with BL (Boys' Love) and the more recent Japanese coinage 'Gay' in describing stories with homo-social, -erotic and –sexual contents between male characters. *Yuri* is a genre term, which is partly identical with Girls' Love used in describing stories with homo-social, -erotic and –sexual contents between female characters.

Venturing into further elaborations of the interrelation between Japanese content and Danish culture, Marie continued:

> This culture in Japan, *yaori* and *yuri*, it's not something we actually have here in Denmark, but because it's not a problem to talk about it, you get this meeting between content and culture, and that creates a very special community [...] Something is happening in this meeting, which maybe belongs neither to Danish nor to Asian culture (Marie, interview).

Marie, in other words, theorizes about a presence in the Danish cosplay community of a kind of sensibility towards *yaoi* that has slipped into the social fabric. She sees the configuration of a 'third space' in which Japanese media contents with their features of *yaori* and *yuri* meet with Danish social conventions of relative sexual openness and liberalism.[32]

From this perspective, the Danish cosplay community thus actualizes Asian *yaoi* media culture. Even if cosplayers, as stated by Lunning, are "slipping and sliding into all manner of identities that have no name but are identifiable through rapid-fire snippets of gestures, manic vocal peculiarities, and poses, to become popular cultural iconic characterizations and quotations of exotic, erotic and gendered types" (2011: 83), this particular feature engenders a performative space, where gender-fluidity, playfulness and various kinds of socialities (including sexualities) played out in manga and anime, and specifically in *yaoi* and *yuri*, become productive. If we follow Marie's line of argument, it actualizes a relative sexual openness and liberalism, which is characteristic of Danish youth culture, but which is intensified or Japanized in the transnational sense described by Ruh:

> Anime may not necessarily carry with it markers of an "authentic" Japan (however this may be construed), but in practice many people now associate these "stateless" anime programs with ideas of Japan, and in this way the culturally "unmarked" anime becomes "marked" as Japanese not because of necessary elements within the text, but because of how anime has become a part of popular discourse (2014: 168).

32 I am not going into the part of Marie's argument in which she talks about the rupture between *yaoi/yuri* and Japanese (youth) sociality, but merely infer that, even if the Japanese convention space perhaps does not facilitate this kind of sociality, there are other social spaces in Japanese cosplay in which such interactions are present if not common. A Southeast Asian cosplayer informant living in Denmark argued that in an Asian context *yaoi* can be a safe zone for exploring (sexualized) identities as parents may be more acceptant towards same-sex friendly interactions. My Japanese informants said that some heterosexual cosplayers explored homosexuality through cosplay. One homosexual cosplayer was annoyed by heterosexual cosplayers who explored this theme for the fun of it.

Marie's narrative of her community experience with its multiple takes on gendered and de-gendered performances speaks to an understanding of this social space as being constituted of 'moments of degrounding or indeterminancy' (Lamerichs 2011:5.4) rather than re-inscribing dominant gender norms (Gn 2011). In this sense, it is a queer or progressive space in which (at least some of) the participants experience a sociality around what Cho has identified as East Asian sensibilities; that is, emerging structures of feeling within the cultural geography of the region (Cho 2011: 393).

The convention narrative shows a confident, vibrant Danish community, which sees itself in the midst of actualizing manga/Japanese media worlds against the backdrop of childhood and early youth literacies and intimacies. I have attempted to explain this emerging space in terms of trans-Asian mediated referencing. This referencing is largely disconnected from Japanese cosplay communities and Japan beyond the point of media culture. However, considering the bodily transformations at play in cosplay, there is a longing towards engaging with otherness in which a specific perception of Japan(eseness) – as we have just seen it to be the case with Marie's *yaori/ yuri* narrative – come together. I will further explore this formation now.

(Un)marked Bodies

During the interview, TinYasuo pointed out how he found that cosplay enables a 'middle ground encounter', and how this encounter is brought about by the cosplayers' bodies turned into characters, which temporarily collapses the borders between Denmark and Japan, male and female, media and human, media industry and fan productivity:

> It is as if people are kind of meeting in the middle, I think, with the way people do their costumes, put on their make-up and such. It is as if you meet in the middle. Ultimately, everyone is striving for the same result. But it seems like

> everything blends together. Then it almost seems like the racial differences become erased, I think. Because when you are in costume, you don't notice it [the differences] in the same way (TinYasuo, interview).

Characters flow in a wild journey across media and formats. The human body is one of these. Rather than considering the connectivity between Danish cosplayers and Japan, we thus consider here how the cosplayer's body temporarily *becomes* something (else), and how this flow is associated with Japan.

The body is a tool of experimentation. As the bearer of gendered, age, ethnic and racial, as well as various physical markers, the individual body has certain limitations and potentialities. Among both Danish and Japanese cosplayers, whom I interviewed, features of gender, ethnicity and ontology (human, robot, android etc.) were considered easily traversable. In contrast, age was recurrently identified as a hindrance. On a side note, charisma (beauty) was mentioned by some as an important prerequisite to gain recognition and popularity as a cosplayer.

Importantly, to the Danish cosplayers, the inscribable body is not about becoming Japanese, or, for that matter, American in any simple sense. Various other aspects unrelated to nationality were mentioned by them. Himo, for example, mainly engaged in crossplay. In other words, she almost exclusively performed male characters and gave various reasons for this: Firstly, she said that her body-type enabled this possibility. Secondly, she is more interested in the personalities of male characters ('more deep') than female characters ('hysterical and pink'). Apart from that, there is a relative 'shortage' of male cosplayers in the community, which means that Himo often takes the male role in pairings with other female cosplaying friends. Enilokin, on the other hand, often cosplays cute but tough (badass) female characters from Japanese video games, manga and anime, but equally so from US animation.

Likewise, TinYasuo mainly cosplayed characters of his own gender, and, parallel to his *ikemen* image, recurrently explored *bishonen* ('pretty boy') characters. While the transformative aspirations of cosplay are not exhausted in explorations of gender, these are a main constitutive part of fan productivity, and a salient point of entry for understanding where the Danish and Japanese cosplayers, through bodily transformations, 'meet' in the middle.[33]

We have seen how gender unfolds on a spectrum in the community setting and through character choices. It is also useful to consider the Danish and Japanese body meeting in the middle as dissimilar from the meeting of two ethnically / racially marked bodies. The media origin is already fluctuating. In some ways, it is the 'stateless' flavour of Japanese media worlds that plays a role in enabling this 'meeting in the middle' Japanization of the Danish cosplayers' bodies. As explained by Kelevar:

> To me, it's more a ... If I want to do it, then I do it. And then it does not really matter whether it [the character] is from an anime or the internet. It really depends upon what catches my attention and what's there. Also, because in a way some of them [the anime] are Western stories, which have been remade into anime ... So, it can be a bit difficult to just say that, well, it is in fact Western or Japanese (Kelevar, interview).

---

33 A South East Asian cosplayer residing in Denmark was by far the most explicit in her 'racialization' of the cosplayer's body and its inherent potentialities. She stated that '[...] because Japanese cosplayers, like myself as well, we have flat faces. If you don't notice, our features don't stand out when it comes to photos. Because of that it's also easier to manipulate, given make-up. Whereas for the European cosplayers, the facial features are not really ... you can't really change anything. A big nose is a big nose. And it's much more stringent features'. In a general debate climate, where issues of 'cultural appropriation', blackfacing and everyday racism are prominent and also impact in different ways on the cosplay community, the politics of the transformative body and its ethnic versatility is a feature to be considered by Danish cosplayers. One informant stated that she was fully aware of the blackfacing issue, but strove to carve out a position for Danish cosplay beyond the political: 'Why can't we just be acceptant of everything? God damn it, we're just a bunch of nerds. It's a bit like this thing that comes up now and again. But I'm more like, let's just not get into these political discussions. Let's just realize that we are a bunch of nerds, who like characters'.

Kelevar's statement nicely brings out the fact that Japanese media worlds churn out narratives, characters and story-worlds, which explicitly or implicitly refer to Western narratives, characters and story-worlds. Capturing a Japanese character with the cosplayer's body is not simply a matter of transforming into something deemed ethnically or racially Japanese. It is more related to the statelessness / *mukokuseki* argument mentioned above.

Ruh identfies various salient referent points from anime's *mukokuseki* nature, a key one being physical appearance, and argues that this statelessnes "is a way for contemporary Japanese to playfully escape their own concepts of Japan and their own feelings of Japaneseness" (2014: 168). This then also became something for non-Japanese who likewise played with different identities. Thereby, this statelessness came to be identified with Japaneseness. Ruh thus further argues that "[...] in order to create a space for Japanese animation to thrive, it needed to secure its own marketplace niche by first becoming less Japanese and more "global." It was only after that that the form could be recognized as Japanese" (ibid: 169). In this last section, I explore how *mukokuseki* is practiced in a Danish cosplayer's workshop.

The performing bodies of cosplayers are nexuses of transnationality, not least in their connectedness with Japanese media as enterprises producing statelessness. Marie's description of how she cosplayed Sophie, a main character in Hayao Miyazaki's anime *Howl's Moving Castle*, provides one perspective on how this trans-Asian mediated referencing is exercised in the cosplayer's workshop. In explaining her work with the dress that Sophie wears in the final scene of the anime, Marie circles around the concept of airiness:

> Well, it is still this airiness, which I feel that the scene kind of portrays. Which I felt was really, really important to include [...]
>
> But, well, it is something that means something to me. Because the film [*Howl's Moving Castle*] matters to me, and it has something symbolic, really,

> because it has this lightness, airiness. Well, calmness, actually, on the background of a very dramatic story, right? [...]
>
> Basically, I think that it is all about understanding characters. Because, by understanding the character, then, well then you understand for example what kind of clothes they wear and so on. And what the clothes mean to the character. This airiness and innocence, right? Which very much is what the character [Sophie] is about (Marie, interview).

With 'airiness' at the centre of Marie's sustained work with the character Sophie there is no intention to transform or alter the character or the story-world. The sense here is not of 'playing with' and much less a departure from *Howl's Moving Castle*. It is an exploration and argumentative engagement with character, story-world and design. In *The Animé Art of Hayao Miyazaki,* Dani Cavallaro thus suggests:

> The closing scene's romantic mood and blue skies may seem to usher in an optimistic disposition, but they can hardly be regarded as conclusively reparative. The audience is simply not allowed to indulge in this moment of harmony and somehow suppress or repress the troubling images of ruination and blinding acrimony that have marked several of the film's most dramatic sequences. [...]Thus, the finale serves to amplify, ironically, the omnipresent sense of darkness that permeates the main body of the narrative (2006: loc. 170-171).

The timing, care and thoroughness with which Marie has inserted herself into the finale likewise does not come across as conclusively reparative. It is not escapist indulgence. It is more the productive engagement of a fan in that enchanted moment when airiness (or romantic mood and blue skies) appears out of darkness.

Marie, like TinYasuo, prefers to cosplay characters from Japanese series, and the 'airiness' of this Japaneseness is quite succinct. To begin with, Marie read a fanfiction of *Howl's Moving Castle*, which made her re-watch the anime. She was touched by it and thus decided to cosplay Sophie along with Himo, who cosplayed the male main character, Howl. While the airiness of the closing scene is at the heart of the cosplay activities, these also entail a range of interrelated engagements. In this case, in particular, an extensive exploration of Victorian fashion, which Marie notes has inspired the design of the character's dress in the anime.

Miyazaki and his anime team have made *Howl's Moving Castle* as an adaptation of British author Diana Wynne Jones' novel of the same name, making the contents transnational in itself. These European influences and aspects are clearly identifiable in this anime, compared with other works by Miyazaki, as for example *My Neighbour Totoro*, *Spirited Away* and *Princess Mononoke*, which are distinctively and explicitly referencing Japanese characters, story-worlds and so forth. This shift and alternation between 'national aspects' are also at the core of Marie's reading of character and story world of this particular Miyazaki anime:

> I don't really think about them as nationalities. Sometimes it can be very obvious that it is taking place in a [specific] country. This one [*Howl's Moving Castle*], however, is a new universe. It is simply so far from there [Japan], and there are these European creatures and the magic is European (Marie, interview).

The convergence of something identified as distinctively Japanese with something in which 'nationality' does not matter is a central part of the link between manga, anime and video games and cosplayer productivity in Denmark, as expressed through the 'becoming' of the cosplayer's body – in this case, becoming 'airiness'. Concretely, Marie cosplaying Sophie is neither Danish, Victorian nor Japanese; her cosplay is an argument with *Howl's Moving Castle*; an engagement with 'airiness', innocence, which has in part gained its substance as an abrupt culmination of an 'omnipresent sense of darkness'. The trans-Asian mediated referencing arguably is at its most lucid here, where the pursuit of national origins has all but collapsed, while trans-Asian mediated referencing, and arguably, an Asian sensibility in the sense that these engagements and explorations stem from but also depart from a Japanese media world – remains located somewhere between being recognized as social and as "private, idiosyncratic, and even isolating" (Cho 2011: 393).

Conclusion

Departing from the notion of inter-Asian mediated referencing, this chapter has identified intimacies, distancing, reflexivities and performativities among a group of Danish productive fans in their consumption of and productive engagement with Japanese popular culture. I argue that the Danish cosplayers constitute a confident, vibrant community, which sees itself in the midst of actualizing manga and Japanese media worlds against the backdrop of childhood and early youth literacies and intimacies. This 'actualization', its productivity, however, is largely disconnected from Japanese cosplay communities and Japan beyond the point of media culture. Further, the convergence of something identified as distinctively Japanese with something in which 'nationality' does not matter is a central part of the link between manga, anime and video games and cosplayer productivity in Denmark. The trans-Asian mediated referencing arguably is at its most lucid here, where the pursuit of national origins has all but collapsed. Danish cosplay may be seen as unfolding on a scale between the consuming of Japan and the consuming of an indigenized (Westernized) Japan. It is in this scaling that we should pursue the notion of trans-Asian mediated referencing.

In a broader perspective, the analysis presented here produces ethnographic data on increased and intensified flows of East Asian popular culture in Denmark and the ways in which this figures significantly in the everyday lives and activities of these productive fans. Revisiting Iwabuchi's notion of inter-Asian mediated referencing, we have seen how the mediated encounter with Japanese modernity through the consumption of anime, manga and video games offers Danish fans a wider repertoire for reflecting on their own lives and societies. Iwabuchi argued that '[t]he inclusion of Asian migrants living in Western countries in trans-Asian cultural connection would be imperative to go beyond a closed conception of "Asia" as a region (2015, 7). As argued here, we may try go even further beyond a closed conception of "Asia" as a region through Danish productive fans and their trans-Asian mediated referencing.

Bibliography

Brienza, Casey. 2014. "Sociological Perspectives on Japanese Manga in America". *Sociology Compass* 8 (5): 468-477.

Cavallaro, Dani. 2006. *The animé art of Hayao Miyazaki.* Jefferson, N.C.: McFarland & Co.

Chen, Kuan-Hsing. 2010. *Asia as method: toward deimperialization.* Durham: Duke University Press.

Cho, Younghan. 2011. "Desperately seeking East Asia amidst the popularity of South Korean pop culture in Asia". *Cultural Studies* 25 (3): 383-404.

Chua, Beng Huat. 2008. "Structure of Identification and Distancing in Watching East Asian Television Drama" in B.H. Chua & K. Iwabuchi (eds.) *East Asian pop culture: analysing the Korean wave.* Hong Kong: Hong Kong University Press, pp.73-89.

Chua, Beng Huat. 2012. *Structure, audience and soft power in East Asian pop culture.* Hong Kong: Hong Kong University Press.

Chua, Beng Huat & Koichi Iwabuchi (eds.). 2008. *East Asian pop culture: analyzing the Korean wave. Hong Kong: Hong Kong University Press.*

Clifford, James. 1997. *Routes: travel and translation in the late twentieth century.* Cambridge, Mass: Harvard University Press.

Condry, Ian. 2006. *Hip-hop Japan: rap and the paths of cultural globalization.* Durham: Duke University Press.

Condry, Ian. 2013. *The soul of Anime: collaborative creativity and Japan's media success story.* Durham: Duke University Press.

Galbraith, Patrick W. & Thomas Lamarre. 2010. "Otakuology: A Dialogue". *Mechademia* 5: 360-374.

Gn, Joel. 2011. "Queer simulation: The practice, performance and pleasure of cosplay". *Continuum: Journal of Media and Cultural Studies* 25(4): 583-593.

Hellekson, Karen & Kristina Busse. 2014. *The Fan Fiction Studies Reader.* Iowa City: University of Iowa Press.

Hübinette, Tobias. 2012. "The Reception and Consumption of Hallyu in Sweden: Preliminary Findings and Reflections". *Korea Observer* 43 (3): 503-525.

Ishikawa, Yu. (2010). "Yaoi as Fanwork: Cultural Appropriation in Modern Japanese Culture". *Journal of Urban Culture Research* 1: 170-77.

Ito, Mizuko. 2012. "Contributors versus Leechers: Fansubbing Ethics and a Hybrid Public Culture" in: Ito, Okabe & Tsuji (eds.) *Fandom unbound: Otaku culture in a connected world.* New Haven: Yale University Press, pp.179-204

Ito, Mizuko, Daisuke Okabe & Izumi Tsuji. 2012. *Fandom unbound: Otaku culture in a connected world.* New Haven: Yale University Press

Iwabuchi, Koichi. 2002. *Recentering globalization: popular culture and Japanese transnationalism.* Durham: Duke University Press.

Iwabuchi, Koichi. 2010. "De-Westernization and the governance of global cultural connectivity: a dialogic approach to East Asian media cultures". *Postcolonial Studies.* 13 (4): 403-419.

Iwabuchi, Koichi. 2010(b). "Undoing Inter-national Fandom in the Age of Brand Nationalism". *Mechademia* 5: 86-96.

Iwabuchi, Koichi. 2013. "Korean Wave and inter-Asian referencing" in: Kim, Youna (ed.). *The Korean wave: Korean media go global.* London and New York: Routledge, pp.43-57.

Iwabuchi, Koichi. 2014. "De-westernisation, inter-Asian referencing and beyond". *European Journal of Cultural Studies* 17 (1): 44-57.

Iwabuchi, Koichi. 2015. "Modernity, Dialogue, and Re-nationalization: Critical Issues in the Study of Trans-Asian Media Culture Connections". *Asian Journal of Journalism and Media Studies* (2015): 1-16

Jenkins, Henry. 1992. *Textual poachers: television fans & participatory culture*. New York: Routledge.

Jenkins, Henry. 2006. *Fans, bloggers, and gamers: exploring participatory culture*. New York: New York University Press

Jenkins, Henry, Sam Ford & Joshua Green. 2013. *Spreadable media: creating value and meaning in a networked culture*. New York: New York University Press.

Jung, Eun-Young. 2013. "K-pop female idols in the West: racial imaginations and erotic fantasies" in: Kim, Youna (ed.). *The Korean wave: Korean media go global*. London and New York: Routledge, pp. 106-119.

Jung, Sun. 2011. *Korean masculinities and transcultural consumption: Yonsama, Rain, Oldboy, K-Pop Idols*. Hong Kong: Hong Kong University Press.

Kim, Youna. 2013. *The Korean wave: Korean media go global*. London and New York: Routledge

Kim, Youna. 2013a. "Korean media in a digital cosmopolitan world" in: Kim, Youna (ed.). *The Korean wave: Korean media go global*. London and New York: Routledge, pp. 1-27

Kim, Youna. 2013b. "Korean Wave pop culture in the global Internet age" in: Kim, Youna (ed.). *The Korean wave: Korean media go global*. London and New York: Routledge, pp.75-92.

Lamerichs, Nicolle. 2011. "Stranger than Fiction: Fan Identity in Cosplay." *Transformative Works and Cultures* 7. DOI: https://doi.org/10.3983/twc.2011.0246

Lamerichs, Nicolle. 2013. "The cultural dynamic of doujinshi and cosplay: Local anime fandom in Japan, USA and Europe". *Participations: Journal of Reception & Audience Studies* 10 (1): 154-176

Lunning, Frenchy. 2011. "Cosplay, drag, and the performance of abjection" in: Perper, Timothy, & Martha Cornog (eds.) 2011. *Mangatopia: essays on manga and anime in the modern world*. Santa Barbara, Calif.: Libraries Unlimited, pp.71-88.

Okabe, Daisuke & Ishida, Kimi. 2012. "Making *Fujoshi* Identity Visible and Invisible" in: Itō, Mizuko, Daisuke Okabe, Izumi Tsuji. *Fandom unbound: otaku culture in a connected world*. New Haven: Yale University Press, pp.207-224.

Okabe, Daisuke. 2012. "Cosplay, Learning, and Cultural Practice" in: Itō, Mizuko, Daisuke Okabe, Izumi Tsuji. *Fandom unbound: otaku culture in a connected world*. New Haven: Yale University Press, pp.225-248.

Park, Jung-Sun. 2013. "Negotiating identity and power in transnational cultural consumption: Korean American youths and the Korean Wave in: Kim, Youna (ed.). *The Korean wave: Korean media go global*. London and New York: Routledge, pp. 120-134.

Petersen, Martin. 2008. *Collecting Korean Shamanism: biographies & collecting devices: four collections of Ethnographic objects in the National Museum of Denmark*. København: Det Humanistiske Fakultet, Københavns Universitet

Petersen, Martin. 2011. "Collecting Korean shamanism for the National Museum of Denmark: ethnographic objects as collecting devices". *Nordisk Museologi 2011* (2): 48-66.

Petersen, Martin. 2015. "Concepts, Spaces and Voices – Exhibiting Comtemporary Korean Culture in the National Museum of Denmark." In: *Korean Art Collections in Europe, 2015 Overseas Korean Cultural Heritage Foundation*: 88-107

Petersen, Martin. 2022. *Hallyu*. Odense: University Press of Southern Denmark

Petersen, Martin. (Forthcoming). *Purikura*. Odense: University Press of Southern Denmark

Pratt, Mary Louise. 2009. *Imperial eyes: travel writing and transculturation.* London: Routledge

Rauch, Eron & Christopher Bolton. 2010. "A Cosplay Photography Sampler". *Mechademia* 5: 176-190.

Ruh, Brian. 2014. "Conceptualizing anime and the database fantasyscape". *Mechademia 9:* 164-175.

Sung, Sang-Yeon. 2013. "Digitization and online cultures of the Korean Wave: "East Asian" virtual community in Europe" in: Kim, Youna (ed.). *The Korean wave: Korean media go global.* London and New York: Routledge, pp.135-147.

Winge, Theresa. 2006. "Costuming the Imagination: Origins of Anime and Manga Cosplay". *Mechademia* 1 (1): 65-76.

Yano, Christine Reiko. 2013. *Pink globalization: Hello Kitty's trek across the Pacific*. Durham: Duke University Press.

Part Three: Interviews

Part Three: Interviews presents excerpts from my conversations with three Danish cosplayers. TinYasuo Cosplay, Camilla (Himo Cosplay) and Marie. Camilla is one of the three Danish cosplayers featured in Part One. TinYasuo and Marie are key informants in the research chapter (Part Two).

The conversations are included here to present these cosplayers' views and reflections on key themes such as childhood intimacies, feelings of belonging and intimacy and cosplayer sociality and to exemplify fan productivity.

Part Three ends with an excerpt from a conversation with Marie on creative processes in idea development and dress making. This conversation concerns her work with the character Sophie Hatter from *Howl's Moving Castle*, which I touched upon in the Introduction. This last section is followed by Part Four: Fan Productions which features six cosplay costumes collected by the National Museum of Denmark.

TinYasuo Cosplay

I: Childhood

Martin: So for you, the discovery of something from Japan, it was, to a large extent, also about you discovering it through the paintbrush or the pen.

TinYasuo: Yes, I was drawing, and I have done that since I was small. I was sitting like this when I was six months old and it has just continued. And then I began, when Pokémon came out, to draw on my own and I've done that ever since.

Martin: From anime or manga – or from both?

TinYasuo: At first, I was just drawing like all children do. I drew animals and people, and my mom was quick to point out: "Ok, people have two arms and two legs, you know." Sometimes I was able to get the fingers right, but often there were a few too many of them. But she said that very early on; and at that time I was about five or six, when Pokémon came to Denmark … and already after the first episode, I was drawing Pokémon. And that's where it started. And then when I was ten, and Dragon Ball came out, I realized: "Ah. That's what I'm drawing. I see!" And then it became more specific [that I was drawing manga], and then it became the thing I was going for; and it was also the time where I discovered what Google was.

Martin: Was it the characters? Was it the graphics? Was it the story-world? I know it can be very difficult to pinpoint the exact reason.

TinYasuo: I started drawing comics when I was six years old, and then it was … I mean, I drew them [the comics] from Pokémon and then I also drew the Pokémons, and then I remade the stories. I think the first one was with Charmander who ate something it was allergic to and then it just went on from there. It all began with that, Pokémon being the best known. And it just started from there and I found it interesting, and then when I started to actually sit and read it as manga … I did not like to read when I was a kid, because I felt that it was too time consuming. Only much later, when I started the Higher Preparatory Examination (hf) did I realize that 'Oh, it's because I'm dyslexic.' I just never knew that.

II: We meet in the middle

Martin: I can tell that Nikoline, Julie and Camilla, they clearly have a group of friends, cosplay friends, Danish, who they meet from time to time – at cons and so forth. Then they also travel around Europe and they know people here and there. But not that many Japanese cosplayers. It seems that a lot of the inspiration from manga and animation originates from Japan. But as far as interacting with other cosplayers goes, Japan is more distant. Japan is very close inspiration when it comes to series and characters, but as for interacting with other people, then Japan is less central. Is it the same for you?

TinYasuo: Well. As for me, I especially noticed the cultural differences between the Asian countries and the European countries, during my time at WCS [World Cosplay Summit]. Because, first of all there is the language barrier. There aren't that many Japanese cosplayers who speak English. And then they are active on other media [than the cosplay community in Denmark]. I can't remember the name of it. They have a specific medium in Japan – just like we have. In the West we use DeviantArt [online artwork, videography and photography community] a lot, and Facebook really a lot, and then we've also used some other media.

Martin: Archive [Cosplayers Archive]. The three Japanese cosplayers I've been following, they are very active on something called Archive. But there are also some other media.

TinYasuo: Yes, there are some others. But it's mainly because their media are located somewhere else. I also spoke to someone who said 'Bling it, but don't Hong Kong bling it.' She also told me that if you, as a Western cosplayer, are able to actually use these Asian media, then you will quickly gain a lot of likes and followers. Because they don't see a lot of [Westerners] on these media. It seems like it works the other way around in the West, where if you are a Japanese cosplayer, or Asian, then you[r popularity] will rise more quickly. So, it is the reverse. And I was told by her that there are many people who appreciate the depth of a Westerner's face. I mean, like Caucasians. Whereas for many Caucasians it's the contrary, because people associate anime and manga with an Asian thing, so that's why it's kind of ... It is as if people are kind of meeting in the middle, I think, with the way people do their costumes, put on their make-up and such. It is as if you meet in the middle. Ultimately, everyone is striving for the same result. But it seems like everything blends together. Then it is almost like the racial differences become erased, I think. Because when you are in costume, you don't notice it [the difference] in the same way. Except for online where people are following these things.

Martin: Basically, many things are being erased in cosplay, right? Gender is either erased or magnified. Race, ethnicity is erased or magnified and media are also all mixed up and so forth.

TinYasuo: The thing is, you can't trust on anything in this reality, as it is.

III: Preferably from Japan

Martin: So you are not a Japan 'fundamentalist'; like, everything has to be from Japan?

TinYasuo: No, I mean, personally I prefer if it's from there [Japan]. Especially, if I'm performing then I prefer if it's from there. But if I get an idea for something else, I also do other things. However, for the most part, it is of Japanese origins. Simply because that's automatically where my interest lies because I love the drawing style and that's where I'm more often able to relate to the characters, as I think they are way more deep than many Disney characters. But there also are a few Disney related things where I think: 'They do have something about them.' Then I will do it.

Martin: So it's both the graphic style and the characters that make you lean more toward manga?

TinYasuo: Because in the West, often cartoons are targeted at children. And there are a few which may be perceived as targeted toward teenagers and young adults; at the most. But in Japan it is specifically for all ages. There is something for all ages. And, for example, *Attack on Titan*, my favourite series, it is certainly not for children. In the first episode there is blood all over the place. And that's exactly why it's like, well, I've always been fond of drawing. I've always liked the way it is made. So to be able to watch the series, just like other people watch Doctor Who or whatever these series are called, then I just watch anime.

Camilla (Himo Cosplay)

The Anime club

Camilla: Manga, cosplay and everything generally [related] is a social thing to me. I never cosplay alone. So, I don't do a character because I want to do a character. I think I've maybe done it once. I enjoy making groups of characters. I mean, making it together with other people. It's precisely the social aspect that I find so awesome. More than … I mean, I'm also more motivated to sew now that I'm living with Julie, and … Well, that we can sew together and give each other ideas and motivate each other and things like that. Rather than me sitting on my own and motivating myself to do something I have to wear on my own. And … I mean, it's not as, yeah, appealing to me.

Martin: So, most of the manga, anime and things you read or watch, you do those things together Julie – or with others for that matter?

Camilla: Yes. I haven't actually watched an anime on my own for several years. I mean, it's a social thing to me.

Martin: What is it than an anime does to you when you are watching it together? What is it that kick starts the creativity, the ideas or just the fun of it? What does it do to you, an anime?

Camilla: Those anime we watch are a bit ridiculous. It's something about us making fun of just how bad they are. And then suddenly it's there: "Actually, you could do something like this [as cosplay]…" and then it's opened up, and we all join in. It's like a spiral and it just goes on and gets bigger and bigger. At the end we are thinking: "We just have to do this [cosplay together at a convention]! It's way too epic for just the five of us to know about it

Martin: So it all begins with you guys making fun of what you are watching?

Camilla: Yes.

Martin: And you end up being crazily immersed in the exact same thing that you ridiculed. That's quite an interesting turn of things.

Camilla: I mean, we did … There is this … There is this swimming anime called *Free* where it then started with: "Guys, wouldn't it be fun to do. No way, we are literally four people. No way! Ah, but it, no way." And then we just did it, you know. I mean, just for one night at a con. At this clubbing [event], where they had these clubbing outfits and then we thought: "No way, that's hilarious." We just had to do it. And then we did. It was so nice.

Marie

I: Conventions

Marie: I'm very interested in Japan as a culture. I really want to go there as a tourist, for example. I really want to go there and experience it and visit some of their [tourist attractions] – even if it's just tourist attractions, I would still like to see them. Again, since it has had a huge influence on my life, on my hobbies. And then I think there are things which are interesting in terms of differences because, I mean … Actually, this is a good example. In the cosplay community it's very common that you hold other people's hand while walking. All people. You've known people for three hours and then hold hands with them, hugging and being very, very social – also physically.

But my thought was: "Aren't there others [other people who hold hands]? Everyone does it, I'm sure." Because cultures intersect in the cosplay community, you know. We are at home [in Denmark] – it's our values, cultural values, our democracy and such. That's our lives. The social thing, I think, is more like a mixture. And I think it's kind of funny because I never thought that not everybody … that it's not that common to walk around holding hands, because that's just something we do [in the cosplay community]. It's things like this I find culturally interesting.

Martin: So you might say that many of the things you do at conventions are things that somehow originate from the manga and anime universe?

Marie: It's not just at conventions. I also hold hands with people when I'm walking outside with them. It's just the way we interact with each other.

Martin: It might be very difficult to answer, but do you think it has something to do with the fact that you all have manga and anime as a common reference point?

Marie: Yeah, I think so. But it's probably also other things … I also believe that – how should I put it – one thing that's interesting is that the cosplay community is usually very, very acceptant of diversity. I mean, very, very open minded. It can even be surprising at times. Of course there are things like … There are always places where there are problems with one thing or the other. I mean, it can be either racism or sexism or something else. It's always like that, everywhere. But a big part of going to a convention is that there is room for everyone. It really doesn't matter who you are, what your sexuality is, what colour your skin is – it really doesn't matter. I find that interesting. It might sound like a strange thing to say that it's a unique thing, but it's not so often you see something like this. For example, the thing where someone shows up within a cosplay community, saying "I'm asexual", then people will just be like "Well, okay, fine." And if they don't know what it means then they might ask about it. If you say it outside [the cosplay community], then you will often be faced with skepticism. I mean, like "That's strange!" And I think that's interesting because you can't really say that it is a Danish or an East Asian thing.

Martin: Good point. It's not necessarily something you find in Japan, the fact that people say "By the way, I'm asexual."

Marie: Exactly. That's what I find interesting that these two cultures meet and yet it creates this totally acceptant space. I remember at one point there was something called the anime dating game at a convention, where people who were dressed up as characters went to the stage and then there is like three characters [on one side] and one character [on the other side], and they can't see each other. And then the one character asks questions to the others, and then it revolves around that they have to pick one that they will go on a date with. And typically it's not a date. It's just about staying in character. So sometimes it's funny what is being said, if you can recognize the character and then they say something and then you know what it means and that it doesn't exactly mean the same as they said – that's funny. And then I remember there was one year where some of the people who had organized it said that there had to be … I mean, if it was a male character on the one side, then it had to be female characters on the other side. And at that moment, I just remember that we were really offended. Because it was really … It was like: "What? You can't make such terms!" […] Especially in this community. You can't. You can't do that. I think to some extent this acceptance comes from … I mean, the whole thing with *yaoi*, it comes from East Asia, for example. But in Denmark it's not an issue to talk about it [varieties of sexuality]. Yet it might be difficult to talk about it in East Asia. It's not something you walk around telling people. Whereas it's not an issue here [in Denmark]. We just don't have it [*yaoi*]. And I think it relates to the fact that we are able to talk about it and we don't have it [*yaoi*]. Then all of a sudden it becomes this total acceptance [openness], because everyone [in the cosplay community] knows what it is and then it becomes more normal that real people also can be into the same gender or others genders or no gender. But it's an idea. I'm thinking … Okay. Again, it's just something that has come to my mind now … This culture in Japan, *yaori* and *yuri*, it's not something we actually have here in Denmark, but because it's not a problem to talk about it, you get this meeting between content and culture, and that creates a very special community … Something is happening in this meeting, which maybe belongs neither to Danish nor to Asian culture.

II: Cosplay process: *Howl's Moving Castle*

Martin: What was, in general terms, your idea to cosplay from *Howl's Moving Castle* [Hayao Miyazaki anime from 2004]?

Marie: I have always liked this film. I mean, I think the first time I watched it I almost cried, because I was just so … It's an incredibly beautiful [film]. But then I watched it again, because I have it on DVD and then I happened to … It's actually kind of funny, because I read a fan fiction, where someone took the universe [of *Howl's Moving Castle*]. Not the characters, just the universe.

Martin: I see. [The author took] this Victorian atmosphere?

Marie: No, they actually used the story with different characters with new personalities, you know? And [they] tried to lay out the same universe. And then I remembered how long it had been since I watched it. And then I sat down to watch it. And then it ends with this image, and it's the only point in the whole film where they are wearing these clothes. So I went to make some searches. It's pretty strange that I've never seen anyone cosplay it [the end scene]. You always see the other ones [cosplay based on other scenes]. And I just went to search for it, and then I thought that no one has really done it. And I thought it could be so cool. I then asked Camilla if she would like to join. So that's how I came up with the idea.

Martin: And who will cosplay which character. How do you agree on that?

Marie: Because Camilla's the tallest.

Martin: So that's easily settled.

Marie: Sometimes it would be a bit fun to do it the other way around, but ...

Martin: But you had no second thoughts in this case?

Marie: No, not in this case. Even though in the beginning, she was a bit like "He is wearing a pink top. And yellow." And it's just not her favourite colours. But then she got a bit into it anyway, and then we chose to do it.

Martin: What got you into it? Is it the character, I guess it is, and then also the design?

Marie: Yes, but also the style. The style and the clothes. Because it is such a really, well, airy dress.

Martin: Well, it is a very emotional closing scene, but then more than it was the emotionality of the closing scene itself, it was also the design and the expression of the clothes?

Marie: I think it's also the emotional aspect because they have sort of been ... It's about finding yourself; to accept who you really are, and who others are. And it sorts of ends with this peace. I mean, you think that now everything will go wrong, and what to do. And yet it ends with this, I mean ... Things are actually better now because we have accepted ourselves. Before they had a [moving] castle, that walked around, and now they

have one that flies. And they are up in the sky and so on, you know? I mean, it's just such an unbelievably beautiful closing scene. Very, very well rounded and they don't talk, and it's just ... So beautiful. And then because ... At that moment, I just feel like the clothes are sort of ... Because they [the clothes] are quite simple, actually.

Martin: Very important argument, actually. Rather than trying to separate the things, like I am, with the emotional component of a scene on the one hand, and then there's the clothes. But that's not the right way to approach it, at all. You understand it as a unified movement, or as something that comes together in it.

Marie: It's pastels. Pastel yellow and pastel pink, and if ... I mean, it's just this incredibly simple, like calm, and then just airy. Because her dress is moving a lot because of the wind, and then you can sort of see it. And that's also something I tried to create with the cosplay ... And this incredibly airy fabric and I just think it was like some sort of "Wow, I really want to create that." You know? Yeah, so I mean, then you start with the question, how do you make it then? My first problem was that there is no such yellow fabric ... You can get this orange-yellow or egg-yellow or something like that. So in the end, as you can see here, I bought this very thin yellow cotton chiffon. It's very, very see-through. And then I bought some layers of fabric to put underneath. So the whole dress was lined with this underneath, to achieve this soft, yellow colour.

Martin: But in fact you started out looking for something yellow?

Marie: Yes, something which would work in itself.

Martin: Because I remember, in the [previous] interview you were saying that you are very concerned with what the characters would look like in real life. And thus you also often choose other colours than those which you would see in a screen shot [of an anime]. And that it is a matter of making it fit in ...

Marie: Yes, it should fit into our world …

Martin: In our world. But here it was not so much about that. It was more … there was no yellow.

Marie: Well, yes, of course if I had the choice. Well, I tried to find a colour which would make a pretty good match. But if I had chosen this one on its own, then I would need a colour which was much more yellow. But then as you can see, even if it is not quite the same [colour], then it starts looking like something like this [pointing at an image of another cosplayers' costume].

Martin: It is intense, right?

Marie: Yes, it is very intense. And, actually the same here. I actually think that it is nice. It is the right yellow colour, but then there is like … And that was my problem. That to get out the right intensity of the colour, then it turns into an egg-yellow. Then it becomes egg-yellow instead of lemon yellow, which hers actually is.

Martin: It is very dominating, this colour, right.

Marie: And that's not the feeling I get from looking at it [the closing scene]. Because the whole universe is so drastic. And that's why I like to tone it down so as to fit in. So as to achieve this airiness, right. So yeah, colours mean a lot to me. We [Marie and Camilla] were also walking around, I think we were … When we were out looking for fabrics, when we went out together because we had to match [our costumes]. I think we went back and forth four to five times between two stores which are a bit apart. Because we kept on asking ourselves "What about this colour?" and then we obtained a fabric sample, and then we went to the other place, and asked "What about this one? And how about if we take this and this, will it then go with the white fabric which we need?"

Martin: So, there is also something about the colours which somehow need to match the airiness which is the very central part for you; which somehow was the keyword, right?

Marie: The light quality to it. And together with Camilla's fabrics which also needed to be ... Because it also really moved a lot. Because it [Howl's costume] is not the same [as Sophie's], but it is ... Well, it is still this airiness, which I feel that the scene kind of portrays. Which I felt was really, really important to include. Yes, and then you need to find ... that's where you make the translation, because again, if you just make the dress like this [pointing at an image of another cosplayer's costume]. I made an adjustment to it. First of all, there is no neck opening. Which is a decision, that you have to make. How do you then put it on?

Martin: Yes, I remember that's what you said. It is virtually impossible to put that dress on if it had been made like that.

Marie: I am not particularly fond of having zippers in odd places. Especially not because you can see that she is wearing a shirt collar. So, if I had to place a zipper in the back, for example, it would have to go up through the collar. Because otherwise I would still not be able to put it on. And I'm not particularly fond of that, so I decided to re-think ... Again, I like clothing, and I like the history of clothing, how it developed, and then I thought: "Wasn't it the case that they used to have these pleatings?" And then I spent a while, probably too much of a while, finding these ... Well, to find out when I believe that this film is taking place. Based on what the other characters are wearing.

Martin: How do you figure that out? Through internet searches or by diving into the history of design?

Marie: I simply search on their clothing in the film. And then I do searches on the periods I know, which typically are Victorian, Renaissance or the

like, and then I arrived at the understanding that it was set in the Victorian period.

Martin: So, in a way, you are leaving the Japanese narrative behind, but return to that which is probably also the inspiration for the animators.

Marie: Yes, I am quite sure about that. Because, it is very clear that that's what it is inspired by. I also did searches on the artist, simply to see if he had made any statements about the setting and what he was inspired by.

Martin: Did you find anything?

Marie: Nothing he said. But in several instances it said that he was inspired by the Victorian period in relation to clothes and also … It is a bit like steam punk, the universe. And it is also very Victorian. And so I searched for what everyday dresses looked like and found out … at long last I found out where I actually could see that she has this cutting, that is the flat part, that very often it was decorated. Extra decoration, right? So I also took a photo of that. I'll just find what I did instead. Here. Instead of making it completely flat and then have to … just because I had to slightly camouflage the opening, which I needed to have. I needed to have it to be able to wear it, right? But then I thought, if I only have that one, if it simply was flat, I would think that it was a bit like "What did you do?", right? But as soon as you put on these extra features, I mean these small pleats, then it'll look like it was intended.

Martin: And these shapes, did you also find models for these, or was it after your thorough research on how to make this part that you decided that this was how you wanted it?

Marie: I really searched a lot for various things, and, well, should I make it with lace or should I do this whole piece differently. And, actually, what I was particularly inspired by were nightgowns because there were a lot of those [available for research]. But I also managed to find a few drawings of dresses, which they wore with pleating. And some were fully pleated, and then I merely chose the ones that were best looking. Still, I wanted it to be relatively simple and easy to look at.

Martin: It is quite interesting to talk about it in such detail. It gets quite detailed, but this is also where the whole effort somehow becomes discernible.

Marie: That's what I like about cosplay – that you get to do this. You don't just have to make a total, complete copy of something. You can also choose, well, how do I imagine that I'll actually look. What'll make sense.

Part Four:
Fan Productions

Part Four: Fan Productions is the final part of this volume. We have just explored an example of dressmaking. Following up on this, this part presents costumes made by the six Danish and Japanese cosplayers featured in Part One. These costumes presently (2022) are featured in the National Museum of Denmark's permanent exhibition, *Cosplayer!*

Costumes is a central element of fan productivity in cosplay. To illustrate this productivity, each of the six costumes are introduced with a short text. Next, they are documented through various types of photographs. These photographs show the costume in the museum collection, in cosplay photo shoot, as well as sketch drawings and other formats used by the cosplayers in the creative process. In a few cases I have been able to also include examples of the original references for the cosplay costumes.

Part Four is concluded with excerpts from a conversation with Enilokin, one of the Danish cosplayers, on her dressmaking activities based on inspiration from the Japanese video game The *Legend of Zelda*.

Costumes

Toshi cosplay

Toshi is a long-term fan of *Fate*. His interest started in 2009, with the visual novel *Fate/Stay Night*. He is also a fan of the anime, manga and design art of *Fate/Prototype* – the original concept for *Fate/Stay Night*. Toshi is first and foremost fascinated by the task of turning something 2D into 3D. Making the *Fate/Prototype* cosplay of Saber, the King Arthur-like character, he used the design art seen here. Initially Toshi tried to create the young, blond and Western-looking male character with make-up. But he was not satisfied with the result. Now he prefers to cosplay the King Arthur character wearing a helmet.

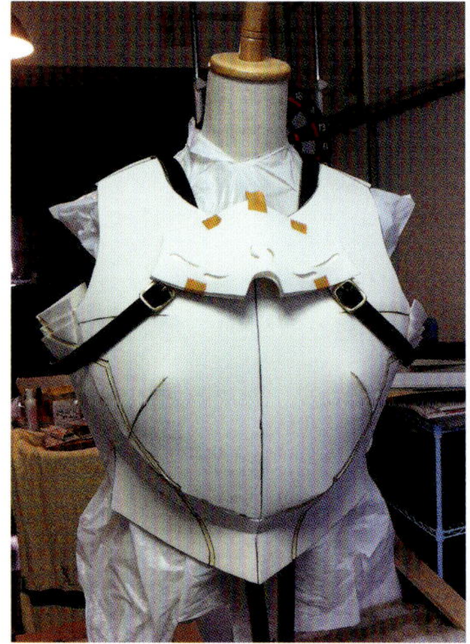

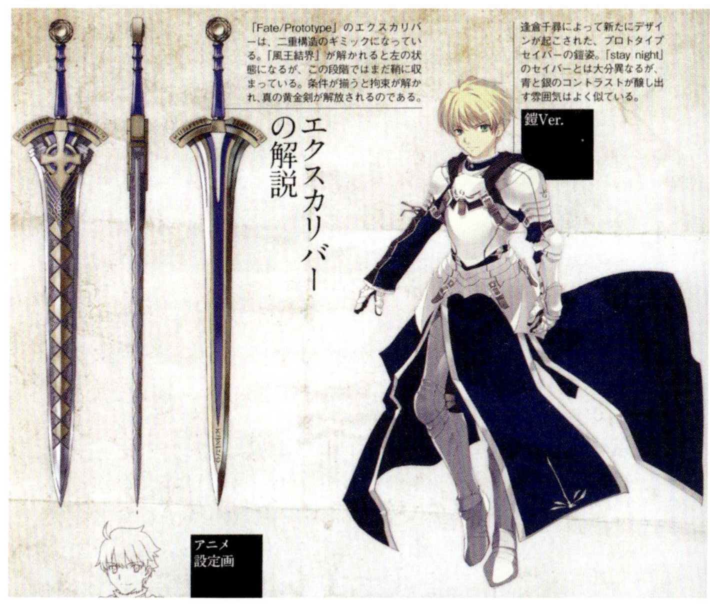

エクスカリバーの解説
「Fate/Prototype」のエクスカリバーは、二重構造のギミックになっている。「風王結界」が解かれると左の状態になるが、この段階ではまだ鞘に収まっている。条件が揃うと拘束が解かれ、真の黄金剣が解放されるのである。
逢倉千尋によって新たにデザインが起こされた、プロトタイプセイバーの鎧姿。「stay night」のセイバーとは大分異なるが、青と銀のコントラストが醸し出す雰囲気はよく似ている。
鎧Ver.
アニメ設定画

Hotaru cosplay

Saint Seiya (*Knights of the Zodiac*) is a globally famous anime series dating back to the 1980s. Based on Greek Mythology, the story is about boys with special zodiac armour, who are called *Saints* (with ranks from Bronze, Silver and Gold). Hotaru first watched the anime in kindergarten, watched it again in high school, then again at university. Making her *Saint Seiya* cosplay, Hotaru watched the anime again and again. She took screenshots of the story and made the sketches, which she based her costumes on.

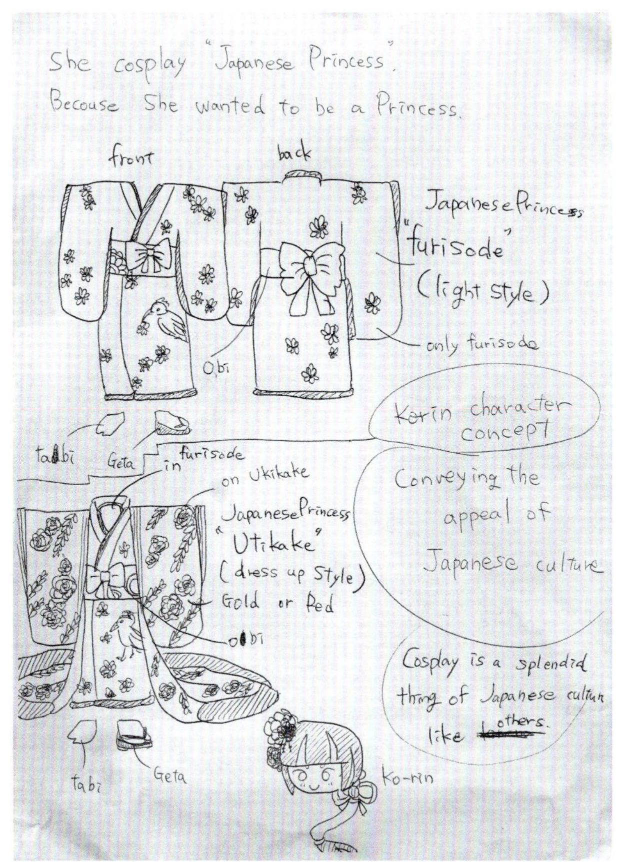

Kurowko cosplay

Cool, strong, cute, attractive and mysterious characters travel across national borders, media and narratives. Popular characters can be found almost everywhere: In manga, anime, Japanese light novels, video games and on mugs, T-shirts, puzzles and mobile covers, plus commercials, fan art and fan fiction. And as cosplayers! To some cosplayers, the characters and their design is much more important than the story. This is Ko-rin, a character Kurowko invented. Will she be able to travel across media and narratives and end up as a globally popular character one day?

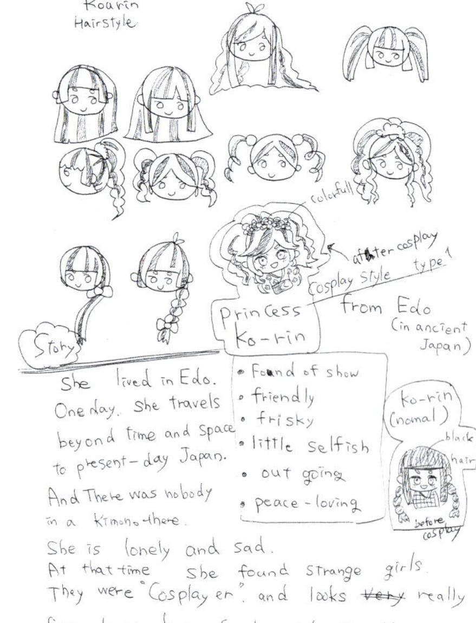

Camilla (Himo cosplay) / Julie (Kelevar cosplay)

"Camilla and I have known each other for four years now. We soon became close friends and started to share our cosplay plans and make costumes that went well together.

At J-Popcon 2013 [a Danish convention in Copenhagen] we saw a music video based on an anime called *Princess Tutu*. That video inspired us both to want to do a performance the following year. During that year, we started to plan exactly what we wanted to make. The first step was watching the series, so we knew more about it and the characters. Camilla wanted to make a prince called Mytho, and I wanted to make Rue and Kraehe – two sides of the same character.

We spent a lot of time making our costumes, which we're both really happy with. We had our cosplay debut at J-Popcon 2014. It was only the second time we'd performed together. It exceeded all our expectations, and we were super proud of ourselves. Especially since we weren't sure we'd get it done in time – or even dare to go on stage. Our Mytho and Rue cosplay has become our favourite." Julie.

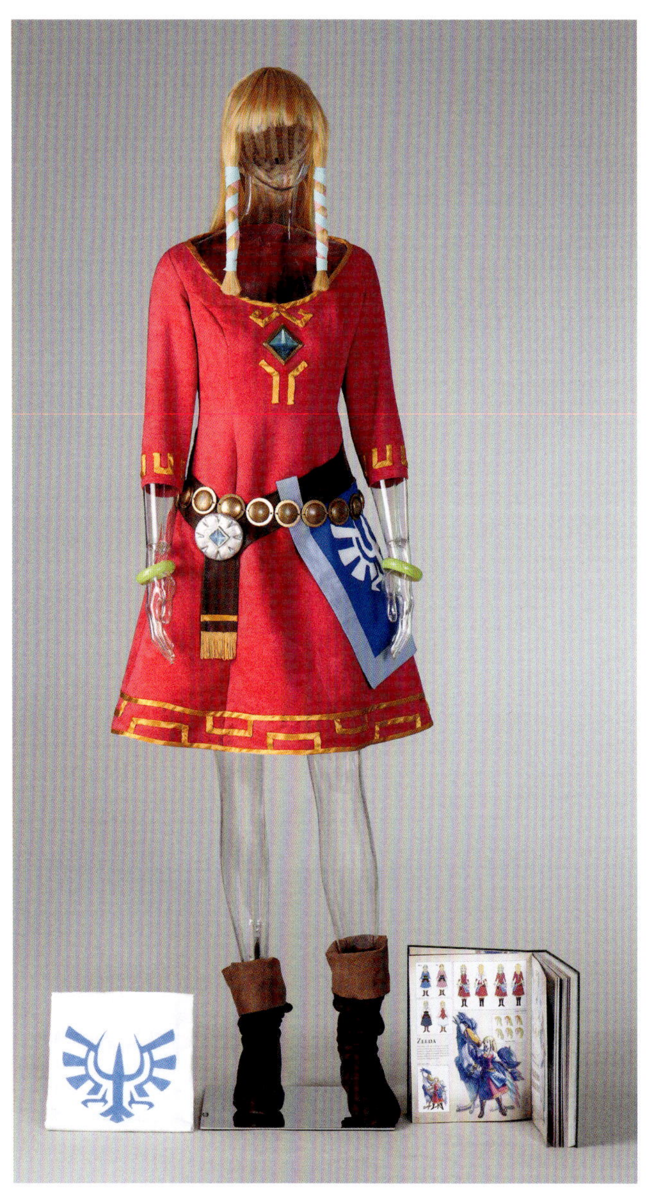

Nikoline (Enilokin) Cosplay

"In the old games Zelda was a mega boring character – just a princess waiting to be saved. In one of the more recent games she's become a kind of warrior princess, and has a really great outfit. 'Finally you show what a badass you really are!'

This is the first outfit Zelda wears at the beginning of the game *Skyward Sword*. I've based it really closely on the game. I found loads of pictures from the game with the details I wanted to include. I also studied Nintendo's art concept closely. Simply to make it as perfect as possible." Nikoline

Nikoline on cosplay and costumes – Interview

Legend of Zelda

The Legend of Zelda is an adventure game with small missions to accomplish all the way through the game. Because of the fan community, it grows. It's like that in any universe. As soon as the fans are into it, it grows. They make fan art and write fan fiction based on the universe. I'm a huge fan of fan fictions that explore in depth and have a good grip on everything in the story.

I was introduced to *Zelda* when I was about 12. I started to play a bit then, but a few years ago I started to really get into *Zelda*. I'm always playing, usually on Nintendo.

Left: Anastasia Cosplay
Right: Zelda Cosplay

Wii
THE LEGEND OF
ZELDA
25th
ANNIVERSARY
THE LEGEND OF
ZELDA
Skyward Sword
12
www.pegi.info
PROVISIONAL
SPECIAL EDITION CD
SYMPHONY CONCERT
PAL
Nintendo

Zelda cosplay

Even before I started to cosplay, I'd fallen in love with one of Zelda's dresses from the game *Twilight Princess*. I thought it was so beautiful. Then I started to find out what cosplay was. There's still one of Zelda's dresses that I'd love to make.

This is the first outfit she wears in the game *Skyward Sword*. I've studied all the small details, both in the game and in drawings of Nintendo's concept art. I sat and studied them carefully so I got all the details and jewellery right. It had to be as perfect as possible. (Photo p. 134)

All the gold braiding on the dress is sewn on by hand so you can't see the stitching. I think that's best. I cast the stone in the middle of the chest in resin to get the shape and colour I wanted. I made the [disk on the belt] out of paper and clay. I glued wooden discs together and drilled holes in them to make the golden discs on her belt. (Photo p.135 left)

The first time I wore this Zelda was at Japan Expo in Paris (Photo p.135 right). I also wore it on a video shoot in the forest. We had a really brilliant time. We got there in the morning and filmed eight hours non-stop. It was freezing cold and blowing a gale but we had a really great time. (Photo p.136 top)

What I like about Zelda is how she's developed from the first game, where she had virtually no personality. She was just a helpless princess. But she's become more and more central to the story. In *Twilight Princess* she's a powerful princess who won't surrender. (Photo p.136 bottom)

Left: Zelda Cosplay in progress
Right: Zelda Cosplay

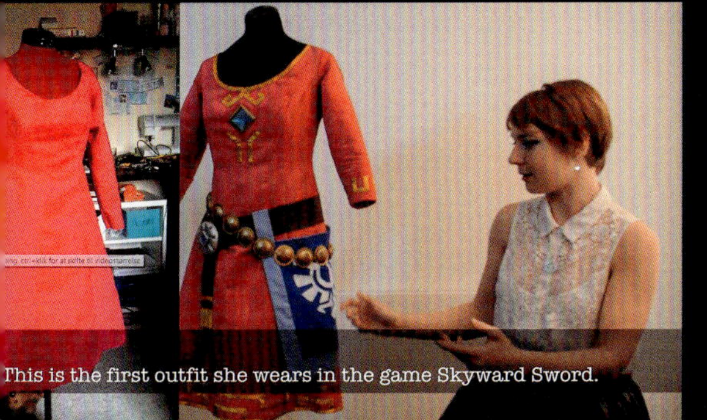

ゼルダ
1986
1991
1998
2001
2002
2003
2004
2006
2007
2009
2011

On cosplay and Japan

When I started to cosplay it was mainly through manga and anime. So I've seen loads of manga and anime. I've also been to Japan. Now cosplay has become much more than just about Japan for me. In my world, you can cosplay anything. I have books I want to cosplay. Even though cosplay didn't originate in Japan, Japan is where it first came from for me. Nothing major happens to me [when I cosplay], I'm just wearing a costume. But I'm proud of having made it from scratch. I think pride is what I feel most.

Future Zelda cosplays

There's Zelda from *Twilight Princess*. I've been thinking about making it on and off. I actually have most of the fabric back home, so I'm ready to start. It could be in two years, it could be in five. I don't know. It could also just be a dream.

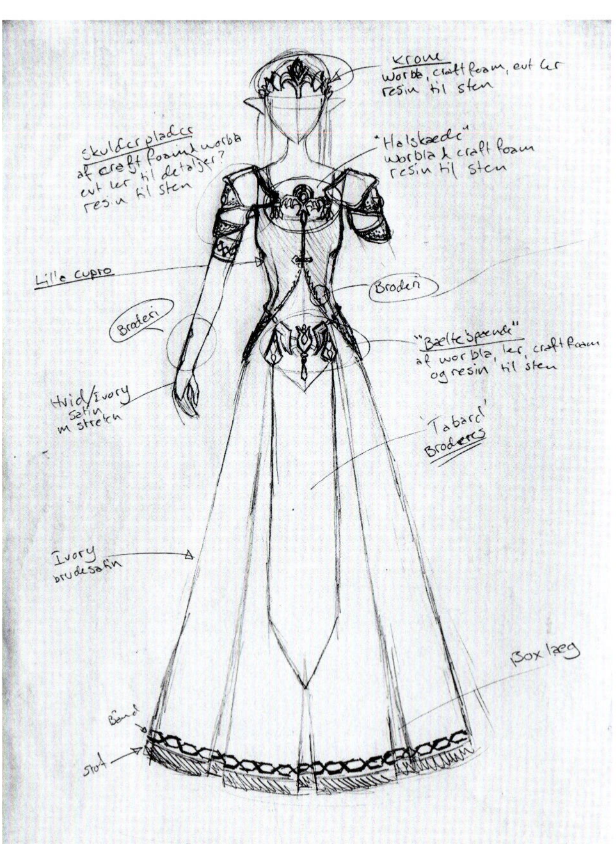

Anastasia cosplay

Anastasia. I saw that film so many times when I was a kid. I knew it all by heart and loved it.

This is from the scene at the Paris Opera where they're going to meet the grandmother. Ever since I was really small I thought the dress was so beautiful that I had to have it. When I was heading for Japan Expo in Paris I thought I could actually go into the Paris Opera. I checked if we could take pictures inside. And we could. That's basically why I decided to do it. Plus, it's Anastasia! So I went into the

opera and stood on the stairs and had my picture taken. During a break two American girls came up and asked "Are you Anastasia?" Loads of people came up and asked. Some kids were dragged away by their parents. People really rolled their eyes. I also heard some saying "Ah, Anastasia". So some people recognized it. I didn't realize it was so popular there.

When I posted the pictures on Tumblr – the nine best from the shoot – it just exploded. People kept re-posting and re-blogging them. More than 14,000 either liked or re-blogged them because they were so good. And I thought, I was just standing there smiling the whole time. I couldn't keep a straight face, which is why there weren't so many good pictures.

What can I say? It helps a lot to have a pretty face. We might as well admit that it's a bit superficial. But it was also the perfect dress against the perfect background. The perfect location. I think that's why. [Peoples response were to say:] She actually went into the Paris Opera and had the pictures taken on that exact staircase.

First I had to sew the entire dress from cheap fabric. I usually wear a corset with this dress, so the waist needs to be tight with exactly the right volume to the skirt. So it took a while to get it right. Because it's velour I had to make sure the fabric ran in the right direction. That can be tricky. The train is made of silk chiffon from China. I put small rhinestones on one by one. I spent a whole night on it before I went to Paris to make it look like a starry sky.

Princess dreams

I think it's the inner princess a lot of girls have that I get to live out in these costumes. And I just really love these dresses. I think they're so beautiful and sweet. Making these dresses really appeals to me.

The old classics, like *Sleeping Beauty*, *Cinderella* and *Snow White*. They don't amount to much. It's like "Let's sing with the little birds" or "let's skip thought the woods". Classical princess. But those films are really old, and the view of women was very different then. If you look at the princesses chronologically, you can see how they develop and grow more and more independent. Like in the new Disney film *Frozen*, where it's Anna who saves the day. It's all about Anna and Elsa. 'Love at first sight?' Well, maybe not.

Conclusion

This book features a group of Danish cosplayers. Being in their early 20s in the mid-2010s, their lives are brimming with narratives, story-worlds, characters, aesthetics and design from Japan – specifically in the formats of manga, anime and video games. Common to these young Danes, and many others with them, their fandom of and engagement with Japanese popular culture does not stop with them being avid readers, spectators and gamers. In various ways, they are inspired and turn their fandom and engagement into costumes and performances, which they share with their peers in on- and off-line communities. This communal sharing continues throughout the whole process, from getting ideas to posting photographs and other fan 'products' online.

The book shows how this 'costume play' in Denmark of the 2010s is a way of thinking, being and becoming in which Japan and Japanese popular culture is something very intimate yet also distant. Active participants in a relatively small but highly creative, dynamic and confident community, these cosplayers 'come into being' in, through and as Japanese narratives, story-worlds, characters, aesthetics and design. Importantly, they often understand this 'coming into being' in the context of their childhood and teenage years as avid consumers of manga, anime and video games. On that note and in this sense, there are parallel stories to the Japanese cosplayers also featured throughout this volume.

These parallels between the Danish and Japanese individuals as consumers and as productive fans, however, does not mean that there are many examples of Danish cosplayers with a close relation to the Japanese cosplay community or Japan for that matter. One reason for this is geographical distance and language barriers. Another reason is that, arguably, manga, anime and video games from Japan are certainly seen as something 'very (typically, distinctively, authentically) Japanese'. Interestingly and paradoxically, however, manga, anime and video games being seen as 'very Japanese' does not mean that they are understood as belonging to Japan. These narratives, story-worlds, characters, aesthetics and designs from Japan are often made for a global audience and understood by the Danish cosplayers as part of their own lives. Where some researchers understand contemporary Asia as partly constituted through this common reference to media products from Japan, I argue that the example of Danish cosplayers in the mid-2010s shows that this 'Asia' is not just something that links people in Tokyo with Taipei, Seoul, Beijing, Bangkok and Singapore; it also is a link to people in Copenhagen and beyond. By this I do not mean to say that Denmark is becoming more Asian or East Asian. Yet, the stories of these Danish cosplayers – presented here alongside the stories of a few Japanese cosplayers – give us ample examples of how manga, anime and video games are part of how Danish youths may live and think about their lives as persons, in their community and as members of society.

On that note, I have argued that through Danish productive fans and their trans-Asian mediated referencing we may try to go beyond a closed conception of "Asia" as a region.

List of Illustrations

31 Nikoline *The Grand Duchess* / Photo: Silas Kappel Staal

33 Left: Kami Renee. *High school of the Dead*. Photo: Julie Rønberg
Upper right: Julie. Image: National Museum of Denmark
Lower right: Kami Renee. *High school of the Dead*. Photo: Julie Rønberg

34 TinYasuo. Photo: Julie Rønberg

35 Left, middle, right: Nikoline. *Zelda cosplay* Photo: Julie Rønberg

36 Left: Julie Photo: Silas Kappel Staal
Right: Julie *Jack Vessalius cosplay*. Photo: Silas Kappel Staal

37 Left: Julie *Red Queen cosplay*. Photo: Silas Kappel Staal
Right: Julie *Red Queen cosplay*. Photo: Silas Kappel Staal

38 Julie. *Calcifer cosplay*. Photo: vw pic

39 Upper left: Julie. Image: National Museum of Denmark
Lower left: Camilla and Julie. *Mytho and Rue cosplay*. Photo: Michael la-Cour
Right: Julie. Rue cosplay Photo: Michael la-Cour

40 Hotaru. *Scorpio Saint*. Photo: Yuuri

41 Hotaru. *Blending into the Shadows*. Photo: Hotaru
Hotaru. Hotaru and Rikunosuke *Just that Moment*. Photo: Hotaru

42 Hotaru *Ogre*. Photo: Rinagi

43 Left: Hotaru, Kia and Nou *History of War*. Photo: Dai
Right: Hotaru, Kia and Nou *Construction of the Wall*. Photo: Dai

44 *Cosplay event in NMD*. Photo: Silas Kappel Staal

45 Purikura in Kurowko's Cosplay Portfolio
Purikura stickers owned by Julie, Camilla and Nikoline

47 Upper: *J-Popcon*. Photo: Sascha Nielsen
Lower: Comiket 86. Photo: Martin Petersen, NMD

48 Upper, middle, lower: *Comiket 86 items in NMD cosplay exhibition*. Photo: John Lee, NMD

50 Upper: Toshi. *Comiket 86*. Photo: Martin Petersen, NMD
Lower: *J-Popcon*. Photo: Sascha Nielsen
51 Upper: *Comiket 86*. Photo: Martin Petersen, NMD
Lower: *J-Popcon*. Photo: Sascha Nielsen
52 *Comiket 86*. Photo: Martin Petersen, NMD
53 *J-Popcon*. Photo: Sascha Nielsen
54 *Cosplay essentials in NMD cosplay exhibition*. Photo: John Lee, NMD
55 Left: *Cosplay essentials in NMD cosplay exhibition*. Photo: John Lee, NMD
Upper right: *Cosplay event in the NMD*. Photo: Silas Kappel Staal
Lower right: *Cosplay preparation* Photo: Toshimitsu Kawahira
111 Left, right: Camilla and Marie *Howl's Moving Castle cosplay*. Photo: vw pic
113 Upper, lower: *Costume detail*s. Photo: Marie Hedegaard Haldan
116 Left, right: Marie *Howl's Moving Castle cosplay*. Photo: vw pic
122 Left: *Saber cosplay costume*. Photo: John Lee, NMD
Right: *Cosplay craft making*. Photo: Toshimitsu Kawahira
123 Upper: Type-Moon: *Fate/Prototype Tribute Phantasm*. 2012, Kadokawa, p. 9.
Lower: Toshi et.al. *Saber et.al*. Photo: Toshihiko Kuwahara
124 Upper, middle, lower: *Saint Seiya* sketches: Hotaru
125 Left: Hotaru Saint seiya cosplay. Photo: unknown
Right: Saint seiya cosplay costume. Photo: John Lee, NMD
126 Upper, lower: *Kurowko's concept design and storyline for Ko-rin*
127 Upper left: Kurowko *Ko-rin cosplay*. Photo: Bellstudio
Lower left: Kurowko *Ko-rin cosplay*. Photo: Bellstudio
Right: *Ko-rin cosplay costume*. Photo: John Lee, NMD
128 Julie and Camilla *J-Popcon 2014*. Photo: Sascha Nielsen

129 Upper left: *Mytho & Rue cosplay costumes* Photo: John Lee, NMD
Right: *Julie and Camilla Mytho and Rue cosplay*. Photo: Michael la-Cour

130 *Zelda cosplay costume*. Photo: John Lee, NMD

131 Nikoline *Zelda cosplay*. Photo: Julie Rønberg

132 Nikoline. *Nikoline with Zelda and Anastasia Romanova cosplay costumes*. Image: NMD

133 *The Legend of Zelda: Skyward Sword* Special Edition CD, Nintendo

134 Patrick Thorpe (ed.): *The Legend of Zelda: Hyrule Historia*. 2003, Dark Horse Book, p.10.

135 Upper left: *Nikoline with Zelda costume; in progress and finished*. Image: NMD
Mid, lower left: *Costume details*. Photo: Nikoline Nielsen
Right: Nikoline. *Convention shoot*. Photo: unknown

136 Upper left, right: Nikoline *Documentary photo of video shoot of Zelda vs. Dark Link*. Photo: Julie Rønberg
Lower: Patrick Thorpe (ed.): *The Legend of Zelda: Hyrule Historia*. 2003, Dark Horse Book, p.230-231.

137 *Nikoline in Japan with parents*. Photo: unknown

138 Left: Patrick Thorpe (ed.): *The Legend of Zelda: Hyrule Historia*. 2003, Dark Horse Book, p.174.
Right: Nikoline Sketch drawing of Zelda cosplay

139 Nikoline *Anastasia cosplay*. Photo: Silas Kappel Staal

140 Nikoline *Anastasia cosplay* on Tumblr

141 Nikoline *Anastasia cosplay*. Photo: Silas Kappel Staal

142 Nikoline *Tumbelina cosplay*. Photo: Silas Staal

143 Nikoline *Snow White cosplay*. Photo: Michael la-Cour

144 Nikoline *Elsa cosplay*. Photo: Sascha Nielsen